The View from 70

The View from 70

WOMEN'S RECOLLECTIONS

AND REFLECTIONS

Text and photographs by INA LOEWENBERG

GRAY PEARL PRESS Iowa City

Lines from Leah Fritz's "The Way to Go"
and "Long Distance," from *The Way to Go*
(Bristol: Loxwood Stoneleigh, 1999), are
reprinted with permission from the author.
Lines from Eleanor Besen's "Manhattan Is
Calling" are reprinted with permission
from the *New York Times*.

Set in Minion types by
Tseng Information Systems
Designed by Richard Hendel

ISBN 0-9745881-0-5

Contents

Preface

This is a book of life stories and photographs of women, all of whom were born in the year 1931, as I was. In these pages, you will meet forty-two women who started life in different places, in different families, but in the same year. They have each gone from birth to old age against the same backdrop of world history, experiencing these external events at the same ages but not in the same ways. The women's lives constitute a story of a generation as focused by a single year of birth. It is a many-faceted story because of their individual differences; it is one story because they are all the same age.

The project was first inspired by my curiosity about how other women of my age look now. It is a curiosity that seems to come with age. I am not alone in making eye contact with women in public places, privately assessing who is older. I immediately realized that, although I had most recently been active as a photographer, this project could not be an on-the-wall exhibit, that I had to find out and write about the lives behind the faces. Interest in the lives of my coevals is also new to me, also a feature of age.

I call the contemporary photographs that I took "portraits," not as an honorific but because they are premeditated, formally posed, and, in most cases, artificially lit. At the end of the project, it is hard to say whether the life stories are long captions for the portraits or the portraits are illustrations for the stories, like the frontispieces in our children's books. Those frontispieces, to which I remember always turning first with excitement, were illustrations of one particular moment in the story. Here, too, the portraits represent the women at the particular recent moment when we came face-to-face to talk and photograph, to talk and pose. But you can think of the life stories as captions explaining the portraits, too, since no single image can capture the fullness of a life. The stories color in the black-and-white images as we used to do with crayons in our coloring books.

CHOICES

Why 1931? It was natural to choose that year because I was born on February 28, 1931. History gives a more objective answer to the question. If you were born in 1931, you were born in the midst of a worldwide economic depression. You were old enough to be touched by World War II and to have memories from that time but too young to be an active participant. It is likely that you were starting a family in that family-oriented decade of the 1950s, or surprised that you weren't. You may have been too preoccupied to join younger activists in the civil rights movement, the Vietnam War controversies, and the social revolution of the 1960s. You may have felt distanced from these upheavals by age alone. Or you may have had the feeling of catching up, making up for lost time. In 2001, you turned seventy at a time when concerns about an aging population are openly discussed and when seventy-year-olds, the beneficiaries of improved health care, survive and strive to be fit to an extent most of our parents didn't dream possible—unless, that is, a chronic disease has found you.

Why women? Although I did not at first plan to restrict the field to women, I concluded that I would be more comfortable encountering strangers if they were other women. But the justification is stronger. Women born in 1931 were turning 40 as the women's movement was gathering steam. Many life decisions were behind them. Since the women's movement at first focused on young women facing their initial choices about careers, marriage, and children, women of 1931 were on the outside looking in. Yet for many of us, feminist ideas could not be ignored. Some chose to respond with a sniff of disdain and comments about liking such courtesies as men opening doors for them. Others wished, quietly or angrily, that they had been born earlier. Many supported incontrovertible goals, such as equal pay for equal work, while distancing themselves from the louder polemics. Still others became activists. This particular connection to the women's movement constitutes a sufficient rationale for selecting only women born in 1931.

For me, as the privileged observer, the choice resulted in encounters that

have enriched my life. I saw aspects of myself in every woman, a kaleido-
scope of bits of my own life in a dizzying array of different configurations. I
reacted with tears and laughter, with rueful agreement or dismay, and with
admiration.

Why so many women from Iowa and from New York? And why women
from Germany and Great Britain and Singapore? I started in Iowa because I
live here, because it has been my home for well over thirty years. Iowa women
were close by and responded with surprising promptness and willingness to
a single article in a local newspaper distributed to seniors (*The Involvement*,
published by the Heritage Area Agency on Aging). Not all of the women had
been born in Iowa, but they all lived there when I met them. As the project
progressed, I realized that including Iowa women was a lucky bet. Many of
them were born to poorer families and on farms. It always makes a difference to be born poor, but in 1931 it also made a big difference to be born
rural. None of the Iowa women live on farms anymore, but most of them
live in very small towns. Location has colored their lives.

I was born and grew up in New York City. Although I have not lived there
since I went away to college at age seventeen, it remains, in some sense, my
hometown. I wanted to include New York women in the project. I defined
a New York City woman as one who was born and grew up there, or who
spent significant school and adult years there, or who lived there at the time
of the interview. It wasn't easy to find them — the haystack was very large,
but it was still a needle I was seeking. Thanks to alumnae publications of
Hunter College High School and Cornell University, the number of women
grew. Publications of Midwood High School and Mount Holyoke College
appeared too late but cooperated with my efforts. A small list of names from
my own high school, Julia Richman, netted a couple of women and, through
one of them, I tapped into a small network of friends from my elementary
school. An Iowa neighbor put me in touch with her aunt, who helped me find
some African American New Yorkers. I wanted to include African American
women because I was sure their stories would differ in some significant re-
spects from the others; strong feelings about the wrongs of segregation and
discrimination were in me from an early age. I discovered that many New
York City women who had volunteered to participate no longer lived there.

Why should I have been surprised? I don't either. It seemed worthwhile to travel to meet them.

The few women from foreign countries are, again, from places meaningful in my life. My first foray out of the United States was to Great Britain at age twenty-one to spend the summer with my husband's aunt and uncle while he did dissertation research there. I have been back many times since. Germany was my first trip to a non-English-speaking country. I have lived there; I learned the language there. As a Jew married to a German-born Jew, Germany is a place of complex but very deep emotions for me. My one trip to Singapore in 2001 was motivated by my desire for a reunion with the woman who lived in my family as an exchange student when she was seventeen, thirty years ago. It seems appropriate for that multiethnic country that my "daughter" is of Chinese background and my 1931 woman from an Indian family.

There are forty-two women of 1931, including myself, presented in this book. Fifteen are from Iowa, twenty from New York City, three from Great Britain, three from Dresden, Germany, and one from Singapore. They are here because they volunteered to be. Obviously, this compilation of portraits and life stories is not in any sense a scientific study. The sample of women is neither large enough and random nor representative enough to permit inferences to be drawn from this group to all women born in 1931. These women are not stand-ins for a generic someone. They are the specific individuals who told me about their lives and bravely faced my camera. Although I name real towns, schools, employers, and so on, I use only the women's first names.

LEARNING THE LIFE STORIES

I developed an open-ended questionnaire of thirty-four items, which I administered orally and quite informally while taking notes. (The questionnaire appears in Appendix A.) Most of the questions are factual—about family, schools, marriage and children, employment, present interests and occupations. A few of them call for reflecting on aspects of being a woman born in 1931. I also left with each woman one very general question about the significance of a birth date in 1931, asking for a handwritten reply. In almost every case, we talked first and I photographed afterward. I interviewed some women who lived far from me on the phone and a few by e-mail. In those cases, our meeting for photography was often months after we had talked.

These stories cannot be said to be the ones the women would spontaneously have told about themselves. I elicited their responses with the questions I asked. At times, I was amazed by how much I was told; at others, surprised by how little memory seemed to hold. Being asked to reflect on their lives and to generalize about them was an unfamiliar task for some women. I am sure there were interesting questions I didn't think to ask. I opted to ask the same questions in the same order in every interview. Other questions would surely have brought forth other elements of the women's stories, absent in this telling.

Beyond the filter of the questions asked is my own selection from the answers given, the tales told. These are not oral histories, nor could they have been. I made the deliberate decision to take notes rather than record our conversations. I did not want to rely on a device that could (and sometimes would, I was sure) betray me by malfunctioning. I didn't want to have *every* word from a conversation of more than an hour. And I thought that the tape recorder might inhibit some women, or at least make them self-conscious. I tried to take down actual words spoken, especially when they were colorful, distinctive, or portentious. I transcribed my notes very soon after each interview. In asking for a written statement about the significance of being born in 1931, I was seeking to be able to use more of a woman's own words.

As we age and finally acknowledge that we are old, we seem to develop a new hunger, a hunger to tell stories from our life. Frustrated by no longer being able to learn those things about our past that we didn't find out when our parents or others were alive, we are forced to use what we already know and what we still remember to shape our stories. My curiosity and interest in the women was matched by their eagerness to tell me about themselves.

I came to the women to listen and to learn about them, not to tell about myself. It was the same when I interviewed on the phone. But often I was asked about myself. Not every woman understood at first that I, too, was a woman of 1931. Some women wanted to know more about the project and about my background and qualifications before signing on. It is not that I wanted to stand, like the Wizard of Oz, behind a screen, but initially I felt that I was the investigator, not a subject. This attitude changed in time. Spending two to three hours with a woman developed considerable intimacy, especially since, as the women's chronicler, I was not separated from any of them by age. Our one meeting was often followed by increasingly open and friendly correspondence, preponderantly by e-mail and occasionally by a further meeting. The mutuality of correspondence required the exchange of confidences, and I willingly took part.

I began to realize that the idea for the project and my commitment in pursuing it was, in part, a new engagement with my own past. I had completed the questionnaire myself, in writing, before I met the first woman. I filed it and did not look at it again until I had written the last story. When I did, I found that the women's openness to me called for me to be more open about myself, and I supplemented my original answers.

THE PORTRAITS

A painter or sculptor decisively controls the outcome of a portrait sitting. A photographer is much more constrained. She is dependent on a camera loaded with film, on light, and on seeing the subject through the lens. These limitations are also responsible for the undoubted emotional attraction we feel toward photographs of people. Everyone recognizes that those people were *really* present to the photographer when the photograph was taken, that they *looked like that*. The photographer has been, not God, but a midwife to reality.

My control was constrained beyond the dependencies of photography. I came into the unfamiliar houses of women I did not know. There was often little natural light. I wanted my subjects to be as comfortable as possible: they were not in a strange place, but my being there with camera, tripod, light stand, and light was strange. I moved furniture. I chose where to place each woman. I suggested, even dictated, her posture, the direction of her gaze, the position of her hands. I tried only to photograph smiles when they occurred spontaneously. My aim was to capture a characteristic look of each woman in her at-home setting. But how did I know what was "characteristic" after our single meeting? The fixed smile, switched on for the camera, which I avoided, may be what women think is characteristic since that is how they see themselves in countless snapshots of family gatherings. Like a professional portrait photographer, I tried to create rapport through conversation as I worked. Unlike that professional, I was often distracted by our conversation, pausing to continue it.

My original curiosity about how women my age look has been richly fed. I am delighted by the variety in appearance of women who are within months of the same age. Looking through the lens at a face never fails to enchant me and later, in the darkroom — under the enlarger and in the developer — I see every face as beautiful. There has been less delight in discovering that some of the women did not care for the results. My portraits made their age apparent with the kind of shock we all experience when we catch our reflection, involuntarily, in a window or mirror. We know we are seventy years old, but our mind's eye sees a different, younger, or perhaps ageless self. Our society values youth — smooth skin, bright hair — and beauty, narrowly defined. Most of the women displayed few signs of vanity. Only twelve color their hair, and only seventeen seemed to have dressed up to meet me. Feeling comfortable with oneself is one thing, seeing one's aging objectified is another. Happily, some women were very pleased with their portraits. I am confident that the reader, out of the loop of self-involvement, will find beauty in these faces.

In addition to the photographs taken of the women as they are now, there is for almost every woman a copy of a photograph of her in her youth. I asked to borrow a photograph showing her between the ages of sixteen and twenty, but I could not adhere strictly to that age span since it proved so difficult to find any photographs at all. This scarcity turned out to be an interesting finding in itself. There simply were not nearly as many extant family photographs, or photographs of friends at school or play, as I'd expected. Photographs showing only the young woman were even rarer. Inexpensive cameras were already widely distributed in our childhood and youth, but not every family had one. Buying film and developing it were also relatively more expensive then. The habit — which today seems a compulsion — of recording every milestone, every party, every vacation had not yet formed in most families. Therefore, a fair number of these photographs are copies of studio portraits, usually from high school graduation, nursing training, and weddings. The others are copies of snapshots of indifferent quality. It is still possible, however, to find echoes of those youthful faces in the photographs of the women today and to enjoy the styles of dress which mark the earlier period so well.

WRITING THE LIFE STORIES

The life stories, except for mine, are narratives in the third person constructed from what the women told me in the interview and, sometimes, in other contacts and correspondence. Not all answers are included. I varied the sequence of the narratives for the sake of the reader, but also for emphasis. I have tried to be as inclusive and transparent as possible. The defining experiences of a life stand out, inevitably. Yet while I and you, the reader, may think of Hazel or Nancy or Rhoda or Catherine as "the woman who . . . ," in every woman's life there were some unconnected but very interesting *other* strands in the weave. At the cost of some coherence in each story, I decided to present a multicolored fabric instead of focusing on the dominant color.

It may be more characteristic of women's lives, in general, than of men's that they are constructed of diverse materials. *Bricolage* is a term adopted by the French anthropologist Claude Lévi-Strauss to denote a construction from materials that happen to be at hand. Not only are the women's lives constructed of diverse elements, but the elements are those presented by opportunity and chance, not usually selected according to plan.

The life stories present the women as individuals. Although the questionnaire elicited information about siblings, parents, spouses, children, and grandchildren, I have chosen to focus on the women more than on their relationships with others. Others enter the picture when they were mentioned as significant influences or attachments. My placement of each woman in the foreground of her story is intended to counteract her more traditional presentation. Women born in 1931 are women who appear more often in group pictures, who have defined themselves and been defined by *daughter of, sister of, wife of, mother of, grandma of.* Here they stand in front, although not necessarily alone.

Women born in the same year but in different places to different families and with different innate gifts; women who have lived for at least seventy years—the same seventy years—but who have been affected by different accidents of fate. Which is more significant: the same year of birth or all the other differences? The variety of these lives is striking, and the collection of life stories far more interesting as a result. Yet some of the same life experiences, attitudes, and decisions keep reappearing, drawing our attention back to the fact of being born in 1931.

There are some frequently cited optical illusions that offer two different pictures: the classical vase and the facing profiles, the beautiful young woman and the old crone. Most people have no trouble seeing one of the images, but it usually takes time and concentration to see the other. Once you are able to see both, it is possible to switch back and forth between them at will. This is how I think of the similarities and differences in the women's lives. This is how I recommend reading the life stories. As a supplement, Appendix B includes background information about the places the women come from, as well as further details about some of the New York educational institutions referred to in many of the life stories.

How large were these Depression-era families? Were there many "only children" like me? How affected were the families by economic conditions in the 1930s and, later, when the war began? What kinds of memories of the war did the women retain from when they were between ten and fourteen years old? What about marriage and children? Were there early marriages and larger families—a common image of the 1950s? Did mothers stay home with their children before they went to school? Which influences shaped the women's lives as they now perceive them? If the woman, when she was twenty, could have looked ahead fifty years, what would have been most surprising about how her life turned out? These were the questions that first came to my mind as I considered what I was about to undertake.

What did girls aspire to be or to do? How did the kinds of schools they went to affect their ambitions? Or was it their families? Did they achieve their ambitions? What was their work history, and when did it start? How continuous was it? How much change was there in what they worked at or as?

Preface : xv

How far have they moved from their childhood home? How often have they moved? Have they retired?

Have they been volunteers? Was it during their working years or after? What kinds of volunteer activities did they pursue? Are they politically engaged? Have they been involved in the social movements of our times?

If they married, have their marriages survived? How many have divorced? How many were widowed? How many remarried? How many never married?

What are they doing now? Are they involved with children? Grandchildren? Is illness a part of their lives?

The women's own words answer the questions best. I have used them as much as possible.

Acknowledgments

Spouses are usually acknowledged at the end of such a section, but I must break with tradition and express my thanks to my husband, Gerhard Loewenberg, at the beginning. He supported and encouraged this project from the outset, as he has supported and encouraged each of the new turnings I have made in my life, and his unshakable determination that this book be published strengthened my resolve and made it happen.

For their assistance in identifying women born in 1931, I would like to thank Jo Brown, Jean Cass, Nikki Cass, Claire Cornell, Jeanne Lewis, Barbara Mask, Susan Mask, Skitz Nichols, Werner Patzelt, Elizabeth Rawlings, Jeannie Sakol, Linda Simmons, Stephen Sizer, Patricia Tay, and Emily Weir.

For helpful ideas and suggestions about the pursuit of the project, its written outcome, or both, I am indebted to Deborah Loewenberg Ball, Connie Brothers, Ira Buchler, Holly Carver, Juliet Gardiner, Kate Gleeson, Paul Ingram, Linda Kerber, Lucille McCarthy, Robbie Steinbach, and Margery Wolf. For help in preparing the manuscript, I thank Michelle L. Wiegand.

The Johnson County Historical Society and the Nineteenth Century Club significantly helped to raise interest in what I was doing in my home base, Iowa City. *The Involvement*, the newspaper of the Heritage Area Agency on Aging, brought the Iowa women to me.

My sister-in-law and friend Marianne Davis gave me logistical and psychological support in New York, especially during the week of September 11, 2001, and since then with daily e-mails. She also helped to dig out some of the elusive history of the Julia Richman Country School with the help of Ann Cook. She has more than made up for the fact that she missed being a woman of 1931 by only a few months.

Finally, I want to thank from the bottom of my heart the forty-one women of 1931 presented here for their hospitality, tolerance, and, above all, their willingness to join me in this adventure.

The View from 70

Cyrille BORN JANUARY 6

INTERVIEWED SEPTEMBER 27, 2000 PHOTOGRAPHED MARCH 26, 2001

Cyrille heard I was looking for women born in 1931 and sent me a note card with one of her watercolors on the cover and with the message, "I was born in 1931 . . . and have led a life of many joys and sorrows. Can we talk?"

She was born in Brooklyn, New York. Her father, who came to the United States from Russia as a very young child, owned a voting machine company together with his father and twin brother. Her mother, born on the Lower East Side, was an interior decorator, a working woman "before her time," Cyrille said. She remembers sitting under the baby grand piano, creating "rooms" from her mother's fabric samples. Her maternal grandfather and his second wife lived in the same two-family house with Cyrille, her parents, and older sister. Grandfather brought her dolls from the companies that bought his paper boxes, and he took her with him to synagogue. Her other grandparents lived in a different neighborhood; she rode her bike to visit them.

Cyrille attended a large high school and had a busy social life. She liked French and Spanish but found math a "horror." She excelled in drama and was selected to participate in an all-city radio workshop. Her ambition was to become an actress. She continued her education at Adelphi College on Long Island, studying speech and the dramatic arts. After two and a half years, she left to marry "the handsome Holocaust survivor, born in Poland," whom she had met on a blind date.

Her husband was a textile engineer, and for his work the family moved to Philadelphia, Tarrytown (New York), back to Philadelphia, then to New Jersey. They had three daughters, and Cyrille stayed home with them. When the youngest went to college, Cyrille went out to work at various office jobs. In Philadelphia, she had joined a community theater group, pursuing her interest in drama, but her husband objected to all the rehearsal time, so she withdrew. In those days, Cyrille said, if your husband didn't like something . . .

She was happy anyway, being a homebody and mother. Her "job," said her husband, was taking care of him and the children. Cyrille's father had perceived that she was a person with a strong desire to please others and to be liked. He called her "Duz" because she did what was asked of her.

The sorrows Cyrille referred to in her note began in 1989, when her hus-

band, depressed after losing his job in a weak economy, took his own life. A year later, Cyrille was hit by a bicycle in New York City and required surgery. Two years later, she had a mastectomy followed by two years of chemotherapy. In 1999, she had a serious car accident and was in the hospital for two months. Two of her three grown daughters lived in the city, and they persuaded her to retire from her job and move nearer to them.

Cyrille had discovered that she was good at painting several years before, when she took an art course. She painted more and more during her years of illness, in addition to working. Now retired and living in an apartment on the Upper East Side, Cyrille participates in painting and touring programs at the nearby Y and makes note cards decorated with her watercolors and collages, which are sold in local gift shops. Larger paintings by her hang on the walls of her apartment.

When I was there, Cyrille pointed out a framed photograph of the family in front of the Duomo in Milan. "Look how dressed up we were . . . and we just got off the plane!" She commented that people "used to take pride" in their appearance. And, she added, she was "quite a looker" in those days.

Jane BORN JANUARY 9

INTERVIEWED DECEMBER 13, 2000 PHOTOGRAPHED MARCH 28, 2001

Jane and I were friends in elementary school, and when we rediscovered each other for this project, it turned out that she vividly remembered all my misbehavior from that time. She also reminded me that she had come dressed as Carmen Miranda to a Halloween party at my house.

We had a few pungent e-mail exchanges in which she asked, "Apart from becoming 70 in 2001, what's interesting about having been born in 1931? Eagerly awaiting enlightenment." After I wrote to her with some of my answers to that question, she replied, "Wunderbar! We'll be revisiting Vietnam, women's lib, choice, et al. What larks!"

We talked on the phone and eventually met in her book- and art-filled West End Avenue apartment, a dozen blocks from where we both lived as children. Jane never left the city (or "The City," as we thought of New York) and has lived in the same building since 1965.

Jane didn't have much to say about her earliest years, except that she never learned grammar in elementary school. Since she later became an editor, this was likely a salient educational omission. She was unhappy in high school. It was the same high school that Alice, Eleanor, Ethel, and I went to in New York City. Jane was also selected for the elite Country School of Julia Richman High School, but she performed "dismally" and was kicked out after one year, completing Julia Richman's academic program instead. She was somewhat "nerdy" before that term existed, not popular but with some good friends. A group of them met to read the poetry of T.S. Eliot and others. She was also taking ballet and piano lessons in those years. She remembers finally being asked to join a sorority, with the you-don't-have-to-know-Greek name of Gamma Alpha Lambda, and refusing.

When high school was over, life could begin for her.

True, I was born in 1931, but I think that it was not before 1948, the year I started college, that I actually came to life . . . Those four university years, for better or worse, formed me, informed me, maybe even deformed me, but never uniformed me . . . I trace my love for the word, for the image, for Beethoven's late quartets, my liberalism, my eccentricities, my pragmatism, my atheism to 1948–1952.

Jane : 5

Jane remained in the city to attend New York University (NYU), a private university, and lived at home. It was an "open" home: her parents had liberal attitudes and never stood in the way of her interests or her freedom. Her father had come to the United States from Poland as a small child. Her mother was born in Boston and came to New York as a young woman. He owned a millinery business, and she was a costume designer who continued working as a designer for his firm. Jane's father died young in 1954, but her mother lived to be one hundred.

Jane did honors work at NYU, studying English, philosophy, and a string of foreign languages. She aspired to become a university professor, but family financial problems kept her from going on to graduate school after college. She met her husband on a blind date and married when she was twenty-two. He was studying law and graduated in 1955. In the years before her first daughter was born (when Jane was twenty-nine), she worked at a "dreadful" job at a mail-order book company while simultaneously trying to get pregnant and contemplating law school. Such were the fairly common contradictions in the thinking of young women in those years.

Jane didn't go to law school, but she did become pregnant. Complications confined her to bed rest for four months. After that, she was engaged in childcare, with two more daughters born in the next five years. She continued with the piano, frequently playing duets with friends.

Jane describes herself as a "marcher." She was involved in the antiwar protests during the Vietnam War and "marched with her children." She also marched to support the stirrings of the women's movement in the 1970s and for choice in the 1980s. She says she was "pre-liberated," never viewing the world as it was to be an "impediment." She gives credit for this outlook to her liberal parents and her "simpatico" husband.

In the 1970s, Jane studied and then lectured on dance notation at the Dance Notation Bureau. Twenty-five years after college, she entered a Ph.D. program in art history. She completed all the necessary course work but left to accept an editing position before she earned the degree. For almost ten years, she edited the scholarly *Art Journal* and, after that, did freelance editing.

To her surprise, she discovered the joy of painting about six years ago. She "couldn't draw a circle" and never imagined she would be attending daily sessions at the National Academy of Design. She claims that she would otherwise stay in bed and read all day. Her watercolors portray detailed architectural interiors with improbable inhabitants, such as birds, butterflies, camels, and fish. She sometimes paints more usual scenes to submit for jurying—"cynical work," she calls it.

Jane sees herself as a city person and thinks she has more in common with other city dwellers than with women who happen to be her age. Despite a diagnosis of emphysema after a lifetime of smoking and the limits that disease imposes, Jane concludes, "We did have a good run, we thirty-oners."

Eve BORN JANUARY 12

INTERVIEWED AND PHOTOGRAPHED OCTOBER 15, 2001

Eve has lived more lives than most people, not only in the *where* and *how*, but in the number of new beginnings. Only in the last twenty years has she begun to bring these lives together into one unified life.

Born into an observant Jewish family in Halle, Germany, Eve lived through Hitler's coming to power and the escalating harassment of Jews, culminating in the smashing of the windows of the family dry-goods store on *Kristallnacht* in November 1938 and the internment of her father in Buchenwald. By dint of her mother's efforts, her father was released with a visa to enter France early in 1939. A few months later, Eve, her mother, and her two sisters rejoined him in Paris.

When war broke out later that year, her father was interned again, this time because he was a German in France. For their safety, Eve and her one-year-older sister were placed in a group home for Jewish children that was operated by a French charity on the outskirts of the city. They lived in one or another of these group homes in different parts of France until they left for the United States in August 1941. They traveled by ship on a special State Department visa for a limited number of children unaccompanied by adult relatives. Their mother had been with them much of the time in France, working as a cook in the homes. Their younger sister, only five years old, was taken into hiding by members of the French Resistance.

Eve herself remembered none of this past, blotting out the fear and terror as well as the earlier family happiness, until, when she was almost fifty years old, she felt driven to ask her mother to tell her everything. Then, after hours of listening and tape recording, she wrote her mother's story as a book, *Shattered Crystals* (Lakewood, NJ: CIS Publishers), in 1997. My very abbreviated sketch told here can capture nothing of the dangers and suffering this family endured.

On arriving in America and after a few days in a grim Jewish orphanage in New York City, Eve and her sister were placed in different foster homes. It had never occurred to Eve that they would be separated. Between September 1941 and October 1946, Eve lived in three different foster homes. Two of the foster families had some distant connection with her family, but to her they were complete strangers . . . foreign strangers. Eve has told the story of the beginning of her American life on a website (http://business.virgin.net/er. kugler/), which she developed with her son's technical expertise in 1999.

She was placed in the correct grade for her age, fifth, because she did well in an arithmetic test although she knew no English. She worked hard at learning English: to write cursive letters, different from the German script she had started to learn in Germany, and to speak, understand, and read her new language. She borrowed a book by Dickens from the school library on an early visit because she had read him in French and thought she could figure it out. She also had to learn to adapt to the parents and children in each foster home and to their customs, food, and backgrounds, all different from her own.

In her second foster home, Eve was reunited with her sister, and they were together in the third home also. They both did well in school, but Eve was shy about playing with the other children. After the second move in New York, Eve concluded that she "could never count on having a permanent home." She decided that she must "avoid creating any difficulties whatsoever" to make sure she had any home at all.

> I was by nature a quiet child; now I worked hard to be helpful, obedient and agreeable and to avoid arguments at all costs. If ever there was a child who was seen and not heard, it was I.

When the United States entered the war, Eve chose "to disassociate [her]-self from anything German." As she explained, "The first step was to rid myself completely of any trace of a German accent . . . If asked where I had come from, I said France." She liked the tasks of walking the dog for her third foster family, something that seemed very American to her, and being sent to the store. She felt "like everyone else" then and that felt safe.

There had been no letters from her mother since 1942, and Eve assumed that "something terrible must have happened." She didn't talk to her sister about it but says, "I came to believe I no longer had parents." In that same year, her aunt, her mother's sister, arrived in New York with her family by way of Dakar, Morocco, and Curaçao, Dutch West Indies. Eve and her sister visited them regularly, but Eve recalls no conversation about her parents and sister left behind in Europe, and her aunt's arrival gave her no renewed hope.

Eve went to a largely Black junior high school in Washington Heights. She got along well but had no close friends. In 1945 her sister was once more moved to a different foster home, a two-hour train trip away. At the same time, the girls received extraordinary news — a letter from their parents, who had survived in France and were together with their youngest daughter. The letter was written in German with a note from their sister in French. Eve found herself feeling ambivalent.

> Suddenly I encountered a new language barrier, the reverse of the one I faced when I came to New York four years earlier. It didn't matter that much because I really didn't know what to say to them. I felt they were strangers.

In her last year in junior high school, Eve was accepted to Hunter College High School. Her classmates were excited about this, not even aware that four years before, Eve had arrived in America not speaking English. Her foster family was also very proud. Hunter was a "total world away" for Eve, out of the neighborhood to a challenging school program and many afterschool activities. She spent the full day there. She met girls of the greatest variety of backgrounds, some very rich, some very poor. She never dated in high school; it was a girls' world.

It was also a world without her personal past. Eve did not talk about where she was from or about her foster home life, except to her closest friend. In 1946 her parents and younger sister arrived but did not immediately have an apartment. When they found one and Eve was able to move in with them in Brooklyn, she simply filled out a change of address form in the school office, saying nothing there or to her friends about where she was going. It was the first time her address did not include "in care of." Decades later, when her book appeared, she sent a mailing to high school friends. They were amazed because they knew nothing of her background.

Eve was "flabbergasted" that she did so well at Hunter. After graduation, she took a two-month secretarial course to be qualified for the jobs she

needed to see herself through college. She became a night student at Brooklyn College, one of the city colleges, while working full time during the day. She majored in history and English, and graduated in five and one-half years, regularly taking an overload of courses (for which she needed the dean's permission) four nights a week, with double summer sessions. She was one of the first night school students at the college to become a member of Phi Beta Kappa. Her jobs were mainly secretarial for a variety of employers. Her favorite was for the Pakistan Mission to the United Nations, in which she attended UN sessions with her boss.

What did Eve expect of her life at this age? "I was too busy studying and trying to make something of myself," she says, to expect anything. With a fellowship from the Ford Foundation, she undertook a master's degree program at the University of Pennsylvania. She chose South Asian studies as her field, hoping it would lead to stimulating work. What it led to was marriage. She met her future husband, who was in the army at nearby Fort Dix, and they soon married and moved to Queens in New York. In her second year of the master's program, which she completed, she commuted to Philadelphia two to three times a week.

Eve passed the civil service exam and, for the next seven years, while her husband was struggling to establish a law practice, she worked for the Social Security Administration. Her children, a girl and then a boy, were born after this period, when she was thirty-two and thirty-five years old. Eve stayed home before the children started school.

She and her husband became increasingly active in Democratic reform politics in New York. To make the electoral process more democratic, Eve and her husband worked to get reform-minded candidates on the ballots in primary elections and to get them elected. They often succeeded in putting their candidates on the ballots, but Eve reports, "we lost elections more often than we won." They were also active for presidential candidates and in the antiwar, civil rights, and nuclear disarmament movements.

Of course there were mundane activities—meetings, telephone and door-to-door canvassing, mailings, newsletters, many of which I wrote. Not surprisingly, I also helped write campaign literature.

Eve had known that she wanted to be a writer from the age of twelve. In 1978, she enrolled in a writing course at the New School in New York City and studied there for two years. It was a momentous choice because it led directly to her recovery of her past.

The teacher's instruction to write about myself did not lead me to *want* to learn about myself; rather it became an imperative. I was always troubled by the feeling that a part of my past was missing. Being unable to follow the [teacher's] instruction made me realize I could no longer tolerate living in a state of denial.

It was a time in Eve's life when she was becoming more serious about her writing and had more time and enough financial security to be able to think of her own needs and goals. As she learned from her mother what she had forgotten or had never known, Eve began writing about herself for the course. It stuns her that in neither year in which she was a member of the writing class did the teacher choose to read from anything she had submitted. She can only guess that he couldn't face the substance of her story.

In 1980 Eve became a reporter for and then feature editor of the *Riverdale Press*, a weekly, prize-winning newspaper with circulation in the Bronx and Westchester County. Her earlier newspaper work as a volunteer proved a good credential. She was very happy and worked there four years. The only drawback was how much she smoked at work, increasing through the week as the weekly edition came closer to press time.

Looking for a change, in 1985 Eve became the press officer for the comptroller of New York City, issuing press releases, giving press briefings, and accompanying the comptroller to meetings. She also stopped smoking. Soon after she took this position, Eve and her husband separated, divorcing in

1989. That year, she met a second cousin, a widower who came from London to attend a sixtieth anniversary party for Eve's parents. She married him in 1991 and moved to London, where she lives in the midst of a large, warm Orthodox Jewish community. In her foster home years, Eve had moved away from the religion of her family, so this environment was something new to adjust to at age sixty. Her second marriage also meant leaving the city that, she felt, "helped make [her] the person" she is, leaving family and the friends with whom she had a shared history: "I find it ironic that my early life was a closed book until I was almost fifty, and now my adult life in New York is also on the shelf." Another new beginning after all the others.

Eve has become ever more involved with other Holocaust survivors on the Internet and with "alumni" of the ship on which she came to the United States. She gives talks in schools to children ten to twelve years old, beginning, "When I was your age . . ." Eve says of her life, "I made it up as I went along." It was a "chaotic childhood without security or role models." She believes that her strong empathy with people has come from her own unmet needs when she was young. She now cares for her husband who has a rare, progressive neurological, aphasia-like illness.

Eve's has been an unusual life. But there are universals, too, that unite her with other women born in 1931: "Wrinkles," Eve says, a "slowing down," aches, less energy, having to get up during the night. She also finds an appetite for doing things and going places and reports "a greater need than when I was younger to sit and talk, not gossip, talk with other women of my age. I find we are all more open than we were."

Heidi BORN JANUARY 22

INTERVIEWED AND PHOTOGRAPHED JULY 31, 2000

This is a genuine Swiss Heidi, although her story isn't the one we know from the storybook Heidi. She left Lucerne, Switzerland, for Wayland, Iowa, when she was twenty-one to get away from a boyfriend she thought wasn't right for her, accepting a "general invitation" to stay with distant relatives there. The boyfriend followed and they married, had two sons, and divorced after sixteen years. He was "too Swiss," she said.

Heidi was the second-born and the oldest girl in a family of ten children. Both her parents were trained as nurses, but only her father worked as one since Swiss hospitals didn't employ married women at that time. Heidi followed in that profession, which had always been her heart's desire, but with some detours. When she first came to Iowa, she did household work. At twenty-eight she became a licensed practical nurse, and at forty-five she completed her training to be a registered nurse. Being able to start again like that is, Heidi believes, "an accomplishment only achievable in America."

Heidi showed signs of an independent nature early. Once in primary school, feeling she had been unfairly punished, she spoke angrily to the teacher. The teacher sent a note home and her mother promptly—and for the first time—spanked her. Heidi didn't like high school; she preferred to stay home and help with the housework. Sometimes her mother wrote an excuse for her to do that. She recalls attaching fine steel wool pads on her shoes to clean the wood floors. She says she never cared for cooking (although she sent me home with a loaf of homemade bread) but was proud of her mending and ironing skills. She received a scholarship to a "fancy school" in Neuchâtel to learn French. It was "too hard" to be away from home, so she climbed the fence and left.

When she left Switzerland several years later, Heidi kept her love of the alpine landscape. She was seven months pregnant with her first son when she and her husband moved to Colorado from Iowa. She "had to go where the mountains were," and she told me that tears came to her eyes as they approached the mountains. In Colorado she started her nursing career, had her two children, and worked very hard. After her divorce, she sometimes worked a full shift at the hospital and then nights and weekends at a nursing home.

In 1979 Heidi received a letter from someone she had known when she

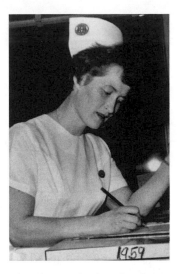

1959

first came to Iowa, a son of her sponsors. They had had no contact for twenty-five years. The man wrote that he was a farmer, recently widowed, and wanted to renew their acquaintance. They have been married for over twenty years now. The sons she raised are both professionals, one living in New Mexico, one in Colorado.

When Heidi returned to Iowa, she worked as a county Head Start nurse. This was very close to being a "county nurse" in Switzerland, a person who lived in a little house to whom children came for care. She had always wanted to be that kind of nurse. She also worked and volunteered at a nursing home, where she is now employed as an activity assistant. She tells stories of her homeland there and sings and yodels, accompanying herself on the accordion.

Heidi has diabetes, which creates many problems in her daily life. She asserts that she is "definitely not a feminist," but she thinks it wonderful that American women are so "equal" to men, unlike Swiss women. Everyone in her family "wanted to do better" and she feels that she has done well:

At this stage in my life, I am content. I feel I have three of the best ingredients necessary for a good life:

Something to do: A bushel of tomatoes to can and a day's work ahead tomorrow at the Nursing Home.

Something to hope for: Day by day good control of my diabetes. A trip to Switzerland next spring.

Someone to love: My husband, my blended family, and my cat, Molly.

Christa BORN JANUARY 26

INTERVIEWED AND PHOTOGRAPHED OCTOBER 31, 2000

Christa lives in a small apartment in Dresden, Germany. I ascended to the seventh floor in a rickety elevator. She was looking forward to a thorough remodeling of the building in the following year. The scheduled remodeling of inadequate housing and infrastructure, in general, is an ongoing feature of life in the former East Germany. But this is only the latest effect of politics on Christa's life. Her parents, she wrote, were aware of the collapse of the world economy and the drift to the Right in German politics when they nevertheless chose to have a second child: "And so January 26, 1931, was a happy day for them and for me, the beginning of my life."

Christa's early childhood was sheltered. Soon after starting school, she became ill with diphtheria and was in the hospital for weeks, isolated from family and friends. At the same time, the Nazis' intentions were becoming evident. Christa could not understand what it meant when her mother told her in 1938 that the Dresden synagogue had been destroyed, but she could see from her mother's expression that it must be very bad.

After the war started in 1939, Christa's sheltered life was over. Classmates came to school in tears, having learned of the death of a father, a brother. Refugees came through Dresden from the east, fleeing the advancing Russians, and even the children helped feed them, care for the sick and the young, and carry their baggage to the railroad station. Christa remembers being up until 10 P.M. doing these things when she was thirteen.

In February 1945 came the firebombing that destroyed Dresden. Christa's family lived in the city and their apartment, as well as her school, were directly hit.

In this attack, we lost everything. Only with gas masks and under a wet blanket could we leave our burning house, and we were knocked down several times by the firestorm. I don't know how many corpses I climbed over that night. It was the most terrible day of my life.

Christa explained that she described these experiences in such detail

because I believe they forever shaped my character . . . I have always valued most the health and physical well-being of all people. I have

subordinated everything to this principle. Better healthy than rich. Money doesn't have that much importance for me.

Between 1945 and 1947, Christa went to three different schools, encountering different children in each move. Friendships were fleeting. It was difficult to find apprenticeships after the war, but Christa's father, who was an insurance inspector, was able to obtain a training position for her as an insurance salesperson. She completed a three-year course of study. Her final report card, which she showed me, testified to a great variety of subjects included in the program. Christa says that she never regretted her choice of profession nor looked for another. In fact, in her position in the State Insurance Agency, she could fulfill her guiding principle of life, helping "many people who were in need because of accidents and other events."

For a young person, when the war ended — leaving destruction and dislocation — there were no possibilities for simple fun. Christa's parents and older sister lived together in one room with hardly any clothes or possessions. Christa never married.

In addition to practicing her profession, Christa was active in competitive swimming and table tennis until the end of the 1960s. Since 1959 she has been a member of an accordion orchestra. They practice together once a week and give several concerts a year.

Christa retired in 1991, then worked for a private insurance company for three years. She and her sister, who was present during our conversation, view the changes in their society since German unification as mostly negative. As we sat together over coffee and cake, we listened to one of the CDs of Christa's accordion orchestra. Christa and her sister said that their pensions have doubled, but their costs have risen tenfold. Women had good jobs and high positions in the German Democratic Republic, and many have now lost that higher status. It is frightening to go out on the streets after dark. Unemployed young people, who see no security in their future, snatch purses and knock down older people. Christa and her sister are pessimistic that things will improve. They grant that there are better goods in the stores and that travel out of the country is easier but say that, for them, it's "too late."

Lorene BORN FEBRUARY 2

INTERVIEWED AND PHOTOGRAPHED OCTOBER 11, 2000

Lorene's early years are the stuff of fairy tales. She was born at home, in a log cabin on the Arkansas River, the seventh of ten children. Her parents had nine additional children between them from previous marriages. Shortly after Lorene's birth, a two-year-old sister drowned in the river, and the family moved to Kansas City to put distance between themselves and the tragedy. They couldn't manage and Lorene's mother arranged for them to go on welfare. Her father, a tinsmith, was too proud to accept that. Since "he could build anything, make anything" from sheet metal, he got scrap metal from the dump and built a boat in which he went down the Missouri River with his youngest son. He set up a large tent on the river bank and wrote home, quoting from the story of the Little Red Hen, "Who will help me?" The letter persuaded his wife to bring the children and join him. They all lived in the tent with a dirt floor for two years.

When Lorene's three older brothers joined the Civilian Conservation Corps (one of the early New Deal programs) and were able to send money home, her father built a houseboat in which the family lived until after the war. They moved along the river from place to place, settling for a time near towns where the children could attend school. It was a little hard to make friends in school, Lorene remembers, but she "never felt alone."

Lorene went to live with her oldest sister in Kansas City when it was time for junior high. She left school after the ninth grade. She simply felt she was ready. When she was in her thirties, she earned her equivalency degree.

Lorene has worked at a great variety of jobs. Her first job after leaving school was in a spinach canning factory alongside men. Then she moved to Cedar Rapids, Iowa, to work in a restaurant owned by another one of her sisters. She married at sixteen—not that she "had to"—and is still married to the same man. She has three grown daughters and seven grandchildren.

Before her girls went to school, Lorene stayed at home but took in washing and ironing. She has worked in sales—including at a state liquor store, where she rose to assistant manager—in childcare through a state program in the schools, and now she works in a parking ramp as a half-time cashier. Lorene considers this the best job she has had because she has time to read books and work on quilts. She has taken "all kinds of classes" in woodworking, art, and sign language. She bowls a couple of times a week and "mall-walks" for exercise.

Lorene remembers her father as a very honest person who was "highly ambitious but never succeeded." None of the children finished school, although he stressed the importance of schooling. Lorene's mother was a "very strong lady" who made do with little her whole life and was always ready to help others. Lorene has found that readiness in herself, although now that people have come to expect her help, she wishes they would realize she may no longer be as able. She reflects that the women's movement has probably touched her, making women in general feel more powerful and assertive and aware that men aren't the only important ones.

World War II is vivid in her memory. Five of her brothers were in the service. They all came home, but many of their friends were killed or wounded. Lorene's youngest brother was terribly homesick. Some of the wives returned to live with the family during the war, and an older sister worked in an airplane factory. Lorene wrote of the war,

> We all learned fast how to sacrifice, with almost everything being rationed . . . [including] coal oil with which we filled our lamps (we didn't have electricity).

> [The war] taught us to hope for the best but be prepared for the worst.

Looking back on her life, Lorene concluded, "If I would have been born any other time, I would have a different story to tell."

Elna BORN FEBRUARY 9

INTERVIEWED AND PHOTOGRAPHED SEPTEMBER 13, 2001

In junior high school in Manhattan, Elna encountered science for the first time and "fell in love with it." She also discovered that she was good at the more analytical math she was learning. She decided to become an engineer. But Elna remembers having had a slow start in school. She wore glasses early and had to sit in the front row. She had difficulty learning to read, to spell, and even with arithmetic. Once reading clicked for her when she was eight, however, Elna was on her way. From sixth grade on, she was at the top of every class she was in and she even skipped a grade, so she was also among the youngest.

Her father worked as an accountant for a men's clothing company until the end of his life when he was eighty-four. Her mother worked as a buyer for a clothing chain after Elna's five-year-older sister was born. She then stayed home when Elna was born, until the child was about seven. Then Elna's mother went into business for herself as a designer of custom clothing. One of her clients in the 1930s was Eleanor Roosevelt, and Elna remembers going with her mother to Hyde Park to discuss clothing. Mrs. Roosevelt shook her hand, and Elna was awed. When Elna's mother made Mrs. Roosevelt's outfit for the visit of the British king and queen in 1939, Elna was allowed to hem the scarf—"What a thrill for an eight-year-old!"

Then came the war. Elna wrote,

World War II taught me loss and insecurity . . . I knew several young men who died in service and of course was aware of the devastation in Europe and Asia. As a Jewish child, I was certain that had my grandparents not left Europe for America, I too would have been dead. Even as a child, I was very grateful to be an American.

Elna went to Hunter College High School, a selective public girls' school with acceptance based on an entrance exam. She feels she was "so lucky" to go there; it was the "best education" she had, even better than college. High school work was "intensive but not overwhelming," and the message communicated to the students was that girls could do anything they wanted to do. Elna did not have many friends in high school but became good friends with her older sister. She went to concerts and the opera with her mother and sister, and regularly visited art museums in the city on her own.

While playing golf with her family on a municipal course when she was still in high school, Elna met a man who wrote for the *New York Times* on technical issues. He became interested in her engineering aspirations and brought her together for conversations with a distinguished engineer, Edwin Armstrong, who had invented, among other things, FM radio. Elna went to see the assistant dean of engineering at Columbia University a year before college. She was interested in electrical engineering "because it had the most math," but the dean advised her to consider industrial engineering, then quite a new field, because she would have more to do with people. The Hunter High School guidance counselor was at a loss and tried to dissuade her from the field she had chosen.

Two years of "pre-engineering" undergraduate studies were required before one could enter an engineering program. At that time, Columbia College did not admit women; the affiliated women's college was Barnard. Elna applied to Barnard and was shocked to be rejected despite having graduated second or third in her class at sixteen years old. Her friend, the *New York Times* reporter, was also shocked and was prepared to write a story about this apparent act of anti-Semitism. Quotas limiting the number of Jewish students were still in use then. The story did not have to be written, however, because when the results of the New York State scholarship exam came out, Elna was the top girl and among the top six scorers in Manhattan. She was automatically accepted by Barnard after all and formed some lifelong friendships there.

When Elna graduated from the Columbia engineering program and was looking for a job, she discovered that RCA wouldn't hire a woman. The dean "read [RCA] the riot act" because Elna had been second in her class. Elna chose to accept an industrial engineering job with a New York department store for one year, after which she spent the summer in Israel, working in an irrigation factory. She was proud that, by the time she left, she had trained the staff in how to think about solutions to their operational problems. Remembering that time, she remarked that she was always treated like a woman—doors were opened for her and cigarettes lit—at the same time that she was taken seriously as a professional.

Although Elna had chosen engineering in part because she didn't want to go to graduate school before starting to work, she changed her mind and earned a master's degree from Columbia. She was appointed to a faculty position there in 1954, the first woman instructor in engineering. Her parents expressed disapproval of Elna's advanced education, telling her she would "get too smart to get a husband." Elna entered a Ph.D. program but did not complete it. Funding ran out for her dissertation research and also for her job. At least as decisive was that she was indeed interested to "get a husband" and start a family. She says of herself that she held a typical view of a woman's role: to get married and have children.

At age twenty-six, Elna married an attorney whom she and her family had known for years. When she first wrote to me, Elna said of herself, "I worked professionally on and off while raising four children." She had four children between 1960 and 1969, working as a consultant on a succession of projects without regular household help. "I scrambled," she wrote. Her mother-in-law helped out, as did an occasional babysitter, and Elna says, "the whole thing only worked because I could set my own schedule."

Twenty years after they were married, Elna's husband died. Her youngest child was eight; her oldest was starting college. She needed a steady job and began a long-term association with various branches of AT&T. In 1979 she accepted an offer to move to Chicago for the firm, a big promotion for her, but early in 1980 her father died, followed by her sister's husband. She felt she couldn't live so far from family and moved back, to manage production and inventory for AT&T in New Jersey.

Ten years after she was widowed, Elna met a widower who was a distinguished chemist at Bell Labs. They married and, after retiring in 1992, she and her husband volunteered in local schools, teaching science—"advanced concepts!"—to third-graders. Her four and his two grandchildren are important in their lives, most of them living close enough to be seen often. They also travel, frequently to historic battlefields, preparing for trips with extensive research.

Elna and her husband were both bustling around in the kitchen after our interview and before the photographing. He was busy cooking for the next day's family dinner on the Sabbath, while she served us lunch. Judaism is important in their lives, and cooking is something they both enjoy.

I was pleased by Elna's reaction to the lively photograph I took of her — she wrote me that it looked just the way she felt.

Rhoda BORN FEBRUARY 17

INTERVIEWED JUNE 6, 2001 PHOTOGRAPHED SEPTEMBER 12, 2001

I was scheduled to arrive at Rhoda's office on 39th Street near Fifth Avenue to photograph her at 3 P.M. on September 11, 2001. Her office was far enough uptown from the attack on the World Trade Center that it might have been possible. I was staying in Westchester, however, and all entry routes to Manhattan were sealed off. We arranged to meet the following day. The city seemed eerily normal until the smell of smoke drifted uptown in the afternoon. Two weeks later she wrote me that her office was without e-mail and Internet services because of damage to the wiring network.

Rhoda is still working full-time as a consultant for the Volunteer Consulting Group, an organization providing services to nonprofit organizations to strengthen their governing abilities. She started working there in 1986, at first part-time. It gives her satisfaction that she is using the skills she acquired in high school and college in this position. A colleague popped in while I was at the office to tell me how good Rhoda is at what she does.

Rhoda was born in Manhattan, an only child. She says that she had a very happy and "lucky" childhood and got along well with her parents. They were in a beauty and barber supply business together. Rhoda was very close to her maternal grandmother, who lived nearby. They spent much time together, and the family joked that they didn't know who was babysitting whom.

She went to good public schools, P.S. 9 for the elementary years and then Hunter College High School. She is enthusiastic about both. She skipped two grades in elementary school, a fairly common practice for better students, and felt she got a "good grounding in the basics." Like most of the other Hunter graduates among the 1931 women I interviewed, Rhoda used superlatives to describe her high school experiences. Hunter was "as good as it can get!" Girls were encouraged to achieve their potential, to do "as much as they could." The students were assumed to be superior, and the expectation that they would have careers was "in the air." Girls came from all over, not just from one's neighborhood, and there were many activities after the day of classes. Rhoda seldom got home before 5 or 6 P.M. She was excited about learning and particularly loved Latin and Roman history. She was "chubby" and a "miserable athlete," but that wasn't important there:

"Hunter played to my strengths." She was an honor student, on the newspaper staff, and was elected vice president of student government.

After high school, Rhoda attended and graduated from the College of Industrial and Labor Relations at Cornell University. It was a highly structured professional program, and there were few women among the students. Rhoda's social conscience—developed in civics class in high school and from her parents' strictures to "do what is right and care about others"—influenced her choice of profession. She was "pro-government." Psychology was the hot subject for many students, and Rhoda became interested in how psychology could be applied in mediation.

Rhoda returned to the city to a job in research for a public relations firm. She was assigned to the steel industry, which became important during a steel strike. She was also going to New York University (NYU) at night to earn an MBA with "mixed" incentives: to get the degree and also to see the man whom she was soon to marry, who was studying, simultaneously, for a law degree at Columbia University and an MBA at NYU. They married when she was twenty-one. While he was in the service, Rhoda followed him to Maine, where she worked as a budget officer, and later to Alabama, where she worked in the admissions office of a college.

At age twenty-five, she had a boy, then a girl within two years, and stayed home for a while. The family moved to the suburban community of Hastings-on-Hudson, where she still lives. For the next six to eight years, she was active in community affairs and took on intermittent work assignments at home. A third child, a second daughter, was born when Rhoda was thirty.

Her volunteer work in the community developed into employment, first in the village of Hastings, where she originated and directed the Youth Employment Service and summer jobs programs for young people. With an official village phone installed at home, she was able to work from there. Westchester County asked her to extend the programs to the county as a whole, and for fifteen years she wore various hats as she worked to build partnerships between the public and private sectors for job training and economic development. After that came years of working with the Volunteer Consulting Group, work she continues today.

Rhoda reflects that her experiences have been similar to those of others in her generation. Women's career opportunities were not the same as men's. Success often enough depended on "serendipity." It isn't always mentioned, she thinks, that married women were generally not the primary financial support of the family, something that gave them more freedom to change and to choose what they did. Of course, that advantage meant that earlier choices took the form of "marriage or . . ." Rhoda had considered studying law after college, but she believed that the "marriage or . . ." formula applied, and marriage was important to her, as well as expected by her parents.

She marvels at the degree of stability in her life. Her husband is still active as a lawyer. Her three children are professionals, one in Boston, two in the New York area. She lists first among her active interests helping out with her only grandchild, who is autistic — "a joy but a challenge."

Rhoda continues to be a volunteer as well as a working professional. She is chair of the Hastings Planning Board and has been president of a League of Women Voters chapter. She was founder and is still a board member of the Corporate Community Jobs Project.

Eleanor BORN FEBRUARY 25

INTERVIEWED MAY 23, 2001 PHOTOGRAPHED JANUARY 6, 2002

Eleanor thinks Eleanor Roosevelt may have influenced the choice of her name. Franklin Roosevelt was only the governor of New York in 1931, but his wife was already prominent as a politically engaged woman.

Eleanor's father came to this country at age eighteen from Lithuania. He attended night school in New York because Eleanor's mother would not marry him until he could read and write English properly. Eleanor's mother was a high school graduate and had been the private secretary to the editor of a society magazine, writing for it as well. Father came to own several laundries, selling all but one before the crash of 1929. Between 1936 and 1940, he suffered from tuberculosis and was away in a sanitarium. Eleanor's mother took over the managing of the laundry.

Eleanor says that she was brought up in a family where you were taught that anything worth doing was worth doing well. Her mother had a saying for every situation: a stitch in time saves nine; waste not, want not; don't put all your eggs in one basket; save for a rainy day. She was a "modern" woman and a "pusher," and a big influence on her daughter.

Eleanor went to one elementary school for the first four years, then to P.S. 87 after the family moved to Manhattan from Pelham. This is the same elementary school that Alice, Jane, and I attended. Eleanor remembers the first school as stricter, but she has vivid memories of P.S. 87. When we got together for me to photograph her, we talked nonstop about school, and she was superior to me in remembering the names of teachers and classmates. Our fifth-grade teacher, a tall, stocky, and severe woman, had the practice of weighing us, one by one, in front of the class, and calling out our weight to a pupil who wrote it down. For some reason, height and weight appeared on our report cards. Eleanor is slender now but was pudgy then, and this practice was terribly embarrassing for her (as it was for me, too — then in "chubby" sizes). We both remembered being called to the principal's office, as only smart little girls were, to sit on his lap and be offered chocolates. Ah, the things we didn't have names for then.

Four of us were given the chance to skip a term in seventh grade if we did not leave the school for a new junior high school. Eleanor stayed in P.S. 87 but turned down the offer to skip because she didn't want to leave her

friends, newfound in fifth grade. (I was less loyal and accepted the offer, in part because the other two pupils skipping the term were my current "boyfriends.") Eleanor passed the test to go to Hunter College High School but chose not to go. Her four-year-older brother had told her that the girls who went there were . . . what? We can't remember the word used then; today we would say "nerds." Stuck-up? Bookworms? Something negative enough to cause her to attend Julia Richman High School instead, where she was placed in the Country School.

Selection for Julia Richman's Country School was based on an IQ test, and one extracurricular activity was the IQ Squad, whose members administered the tests to incoming students. Eleanor was a member. She remembers the school fondly as "like a little private school," with some trips to see plays. She was fairly popular and active. She once ran for student government and used one of the Campbell's Soup "Campbell Kids" as her logo since, with her round face, she resembled him. She started writing humorous poetry, which she still does, and was also published in the literary magazine, the *Bluebird*. She wanted to become a writer.

After high school, Eleanor went to Hunter College, one of the city colleges. Her parents believed that you only went away to college if you couldn't get into one of the city colleges. Eleanor majored in English and minored in education, did her student teaching, and prepared for a teaching career. Contemplating being born at a later time, Eleanor says that she might have pursued her ambition to write. When she was twenty, it would have been "frivolous" to consider it.

Eleanor taught before she was married and afterward, until pregnant with her first child. She then stayed at home for eight years, until the youngest of her three children was three and she was thirty-three. She and her husband lived in Westchester, and she started substitute teaching as a way of getting out and meeting people. When her mother asked her why she was leaving her children so young to go to work, she responded, "I have a career."

Through a "fluke," Eleanor was hired to replace an art teacher who had become sick. She taught art to pupils in kindergarten through sixth grade, but she wasn't permitted to use the materials of the teacher who had been replaced. Eleanor had to improvise, sometimes baking cookies with the sixth graders as "art." This temporary assignment led to a permanent job teaching second grade in her children's school. She took her youngest, not yet in school, to the Ossining Children's Center, the oldest care center in Westchester County. Later she served on its board. Eleanor taught at that school until it was closed and renovated for administrative offices. She then moved to another school, teaching fourth and fifth grades until she retired in 1992. The Ossining school system served a racially mixed population, which she says was good for the children, including hers.

She found time to earn a master's degree in the mid- to late 1960s, attending classes after school and evenings. She earned "over a hundred credits" in courses after that and is now taking an art course. Eleanor has continued to write poetry and wants to collect her poems, at least for the family, which now includes the three grown children, all living in and around New York, and four grandchildren. I was delighted to find a poem by Eleanor in the "Metropolitan Diary" feature of the *New York Times* in June 2001. Titled "Manhattan Is Calling," the poem expresses the pull of the city on empty-nest suburbanites.

> The deck is creaking
> The faucet is leaking
> The lawn needs seeding
> The bushes need weeding
>
> The mold is creeping
> The chimney needs sweeping
> The trees need pruning
> The piano needs tuning
>
> .   .   .   .   .

The city is calling
Resistance is falling

The children long gone
It's time to move on . . .

Jan BORN MARCH 10

INTERVIEWED AND PHOTOGRAPHED JULY 30, 2000

Jan was an only child, perhaps, she thinks, because her parents married relatively late. Her father was an auditor, first for an Iowa county, then for the state, and the small family moved with him on his assignments, living in rooming houses for months at a time. He then became a tax accountant for four counties, and the family settled in Mason City, Iowa. Jan's father had a flair for figures but hadn't gone to college; he was "adamant" that Jan should go on with her schooling.

In high school, Jan was a good student and liked school, although it was somewhat cliquish. The high school building also housed a two-year college, and many of those students were World War II veterans. English was her favorite subject, as taught by a stern, old, but very effective teacher. Jan was also a good athlete, but there were no opportunities for girls to participate in sports. She went to games with her friends after "spread" parties, for which the girls' mothers took turns making "spreads." She was in scouting "as far as you could go" and was a counselor at Girl Scout camp.

Outside of school, Jan helped in her father's accounting office from the age of twelve and through high school, preferring that work to helping her mother at home. Her mother minded this preference some, and Jan's husband had to teach her how to cook as a result of it. But Jan admired her father for "who and what he was" and for his stimulating her love of sports.

Jan went away to attend a liberal arts college, Grinnell, intending to major in English. Dorm rules were very strict. Curfew was at 7:30 P.M. on weeknights and 10:30 P.M. weekends. It was possible, she admits, to let latecomers in through a first-floor window. Grinnell attracted out-of-state students, and all Jan's roommates and many other students were from Chicago. Jan found them worldly and thought them rich. She visited some of them in their homes.

After her second year, her father had the first of six heart attacks. Jan took a year off to run his business, although he didn't want her to interrupt her education. She knew what the accounting practice required from her years of working there, and she insisted. When Jan returned to college, it was to the University of Iowa, one of the state universities. She had become interested in politics during her year off — the year of Eisenhower's campaign and

election — and chose a new major: political science. She took all the courses the department offered and supported herself with various jobs.

After graduating, Jan considered a career with the Central Intelligence Agency. She had passed all the requirements when she was "sidetracked by falling in love." The object of her affection, and her husband to this day, was a local policeman. She met him when he came into the bar where she was having a beer — legally — to check IDs. Her parents disapproved of her choice. He was "Catholic, a policeman, and a Democrat," "not at all what [her mother] had in mind" for her! They had four children and now have twelve grandchildren, all living quite close by. In the 1960s, when the police were reviled by war protesters, Jan's children, then in high school, had to hear "terrible things" from some fellow students because their father was a policeman.

Jan always worked, even when the children were small, returning to her job six weeks after each of her babies was born. She worked for a federal agricultural office and in a law office during tax seasons. She loved her job in the county sheriff's office, although she remarked that she and the other women were paid less than men doing similar, or lesser, jobs. She retired after ten years, when her husband retired from the police force. In 1999 a special day was proclaimed in honor of her husband. Jan is very proud of him but says she was often referred to merely as his wife, or as her children's mother. She never seemed to be known as just herself.

Jan is a breast cancer survivor and a diabetic since 1985. Diabetes has slowed her down but hasn't kept her from using her keen mind. She is a voracious reader. She still loves sports, enjoying them on TV or as played by her grandchildren.

About the influence of being born in 1931, Jan wrote,

I grew up respecting money, what it took to earn it and the value of saving.

World War II gave [us] . . . a sense of pride in our country. It brought the reality of war to us at an early age and we saw first hand that sacrifice is sometimes necessary for the national good.

Rosemary BORN APRIL 29

INTERVIEWED AND PHOTOGRAPHED OCTOBER 14, 2001

Rosemary wrote that there were few "artificial means of entertainment" for children born in 1931 and yet "we were never BORED and I still am very rarely bored."

Rosemary's parents met while traveling to work by train every day. They worked in the offices of different insurance companies in London. Women were not permitted to work after marriage, but Rosemary's mother continued in her job for a while by not disclosing her married state. Five years after they were married, they had a son and one year later, Rosemary. Rosemary was born at home with a midwife: "Mother was used to it by then." The family moved to their first house in Middlesex in northwest London, where Rosemary started school.

When the war began in September 1939, her father's office was moved to Devon in the far southwest of England. Rosemary begins her war recollections by saying, "I had a good war." Her family lived in a beautiful place at the sea, and she and her brother "walked miles over the Downs and to the beach" and wandered about freely until the evacuation of British forces from Dunkirk in June 1940. She remembers fishermen, whom she knew, going off in their fishing boats to Dunkirk. After that, the beach was out of bounds and the family was on the front lines.

Her father wanted to enlist, but his firm, where he was doing the work of three or four, refused to let him. He joined the Home Guard as an officer and was working on demolition service when a hotel, used for convalescing Air Force officers, was bombed out after several tries, as was a local church full of children at Sunday school. Two of Rosemary's school friends were killed. Her father didn't talk about it but was, for some time, very affected by what he had experienced. Rosemary shrugged and said, "We got used to being bombed."

One benefit for the family was that Father could choose the members of his Home Guard platoon. He chose the local fishmonger, butcher, and grocer, among others. As a result, the family always had enough food. In peacetime, he was a man of "extreme honesty," forbidding the children to use his firm's pencils and pads. His standards adapted to wartime conditions to provide for his family.

In 1943, when Rosemary was twelve, her parents sent her to boarding

school, which she attended until she was seventeen. Her parents were concerned that Rosemary's secondary education would be disrupted when the war ended and they moved back to Middlesex. They did indeed move back into the house they had left behind. Friends who had been bombed out had lived there in their absence.

Rosemary loved boarding school. She was a happy child who fit in almost anywhere. She was homesick only for the first three weeks. Among other unfamiliar things, she hated the porridge served and "wept buckets" into it until, one cold day, corn flakes were served instead and she began to see the point of hot porridge. Her school reports said that she was "cheerful and helpful but too noisy." She came across as lighthearted but says she kept her innermost feelings to herself. Home was several hours removed by train, and Rosemary saw her parents only three times a year.

Rosemary's first job after school was as a clerk at the Bank of England. In her first week, she was sent to be trained to punch Hollerith cards. She is amused to recall that her reaction to the punch cards, which became the first computer medium, was, "I can't see any future in punching holes in cardboard!" She was accepted for training as a secretary because her spelling was better than the other applicants'.

Rosemary sees herself as someone who has always spoken her mind and felt no need to go along with the "establishment." In fact, she admits to a "bolshie" side, an expression which refers not to Bolshevik politics but to never wanting to "obey silly rules." But she has a "moral attitude" as well and felt that she should stay at her job two years after receiving secretarial training. When she gave notice, her supervisor acknowledged that "you need to spread your wings."

In a later job as a payroll clerk, Rosemary circumvented a "silly rule" that checks over a specified amount had to be signed by the director. Rosemary simply prepared two checks, each under that amount. Her boss told her, "You're being logical—women are not supposed to be logical." She says it was intended as a joke.

When she was twenty-five, Rosemary married a man she met through friends at a tennis club. They had three daughters in ten years and Rosemary stayed home, returning to work part-time in 1971, when she foresaw the end of her marriage. The youngest girl was three and Rosemary's mother, who had come to live with her in a "granny flat" after Rosemary's father died, looked after the child when the girl wasn't in playschool. The divorce came in 1975, and Rosemary remarried four years later, acquiring three stepchildren whose ages fit in with those of her two younger girls. It was a big household and Rosemary stayed home for a few years. Then she began a long career as a temp because she wanted only part-time work. She studied at night for a bookkeeping certificate at this time. In every temporary job she held, Rosemary was asked to stay on permanently but always refused to work full-time.

After seven years of her second marriage, Rosemary was widowed. Continuing her work as a temp in many settings, she learned to use a computer and finally, just under age sixty, she accepted an offer to stay full-time and become the secretary to a director of a security installation firm. Shortly after, she married a man she met singing in a choir. The new marriage and her mother's final illness led Rosemary to retire. At the farewell party at work, she was asked if she was "doing anything next week," and she stayed on, again as a temp, for some months.

Finally retired, Rosemary enjoys singing, country dancing, knitting, theater, swimming, and aerobics. She wrote with some pride that when she was following her young grandson in the swimming pool, "doing a passable crawl," he commented, "you're not like other grannies, they wear funny hats and swim like this . . . [his head up, doing a feeble breaststroke]."

Fran BORN MAY 11

INTERVIEWED JUNE 27, 2001 PHOTOGRAPHED NOVEMBER 14, 2001

Fran has lived a life governed by idealism and spiritual seeking, daring to go beyond conventional expectations of women. But she only became this kind of person gradually.

Both of Fran's parents came to the United States at sixteen years of age, he from Russia after the revolution, she from an orphanage in France where her widowed mother had placed her and her sister. Fran remembers her parents as "impatient to be American." Her father worked at various jobs — in factories, as a truck and taxi driver, as a furrier — and generally worked two jobs at a time to support his family. Fran's mother worked as a seamstress, staying home only when Fran and her sister were small, in the absence of childcare.

Fran remembers her mother, always worried about survival and security, pushing her to date young, apprehensive when Fran did well in school that she would be too smart for someone to want to marry. Yet in an appreciation she wrote about her mother after her mother's death in 1985, Fran remembers not only an anxious woman but also a lively one, the center of attention, singing, dancing, "thriv[ing] on people." Fran, too, loves to dance to this day — all kinds of dancing — and it connects her to her mother. But she regrets that she never learned more than fragments of her mother's story.

Fran started school in the Bronx already knowing how to read, but she moved with her family to a small town in upstate New York when she was eight, returning to the city at thirteen. Those were difficult years: Fran was teased and treated "as if [she] came from Mars" because she was one of the very few Jews who lived there. Perhaps it helped her to accept being "different."

Back in New York, Fran was accepted by Hunter College High School because, she says, she was very good in math. English was her worst subject: "I didn't know how to write because I didn't know how to think." She regularly worked after school: as a babysitter, in a doctor's office, and in a candy store. She had to wear work clothes to school — most conspicuously, a white blouse — and so looked different from the other girls. She was annoyed that the yearbook editors selected the Byron quote "She walks in beauty" for her. Fran insisted on submitting her own quotation ("The best part of beauty is that which no picture can express"), but it got garbled in printing.

When Fran was eight, her ambition was to be a secretary . . . Secretary of State! She was told this was impossible. In high school, she wanted to be another Madame Curie and was president of the Physics Club one term. She attended Brooklyn College after high school but could not pursue her interest in science because science labs were always scheduled for afternoons and she took her classes in the mornings so that she could work afternoons. She left college after two years to marry.

Before her first child was born in 1954, Fran followed her husband to Texas, where he was in the Air Force. There she worked as a legal secretary. When he was sent to Korea, Fran returned to New York and the same kind of position. She loved the work. Her second child was born in 1956 and the third in 1960. In 1957 she returned to college in Bridgeport, Connecticut, near where she lived, and for five years took one class a term. She was studying history but didn't complete her degree. Fran says she was still "sound asleep" until then. She came to realize that what she wanted was "to make peace in the world" and that school and the study of history didn't give her the answers she sought.

She began a long spiritual quest, starting with eight years of study at the Gurdjieff Institute in New York. Gurdjieff was a Russian mystic. For a wife and mother to undertake this kind of study was unusual at the time, and her husband wasn't happy about it. He had overcome his concerns when she attended college in Bridgeport, agreeing to watch the children on the evenings that she was away, but he found her studies in New York in the 1960s too much. They were divorced in 1969 and he remarried. He died six years later. Fran says he was a good man.

Meanwhile, Fran and her fellow seekers brought a Buddhist monk to New York in order to study with him. With some changes in teachers, she was in Buddhist practice until 1993. She is now a committed Christian Scientist.

Despite the changes in her belief systems, she remains devoted to the pursuit of peace and justice. She notes that she made her choices before society's views about the role of women had changed,

> . . . and without the support of my family and community. To have that support would certainly have made my life easier. However, it is precisely because that support was absent that I had to be absolutely clear about my commitment to a path of spiritual growth because I knew the price I would have to pay for it.

A young woman she met recently at a peace demonstration called Fran a "pioneer" and said she had made the way easier for those who came after. This tribute touches Fran deeply.

After her divorce, Fran had to decide what to do next. In a "lightbulb moment," she entered a nursing program and earned an associate's degree, graduating second in her class. She worked at a hospital in Bridgeport, then moved to New York with her younger daughter, where she did private-duty nursing — and office work as a temp for "comic relief." One bookkeeping job could have become permanent and full-time, but Fran wanted enough time for meditating. During her years as a nurse, Fran wrote poems inspired by her patients and has since self-published a volume of poetry, *Peel Me a Star*.

She moved once more out of the city and worked as the "token Buddhist" for an interfaith peace and justice organization for several years. Then came another turning point, which brought together her nursing, the idealism she was "born with," and her creativity. In 1993 Fran signed on with Dr. Patch Adams for a group trip to Russia to "clown" in children's hospitals, orphanages, reform schools, and in public. She then entered a volunteer clown-doctor program at Stamford Hospital in Connecticut, taking on the persona of Doctor Do Little. She worked with patients there for a few years, coming to realize that clowning is not only about being funny but also about letting ourselves and others feel the full range of our emotions as a path to healing.

Fran decided to complete her B.A. in 1997. She returned to Bridgeport University where, because of credits previously earned, she was only required to take one senior seminar. Her term paper, "Spirituality in the Workplace," won the award for the best paper written in her program for that semester.

Fran suffered from clinical depression in the late 1990s and moved to Richmond, Virginia, in 1999 to be closer to her two daughters and son, who were concerned about her. She was healed by a Christian Science practitioner after a variety of medications failed to help, and then converted to Christian Science. Fran has now combined clowning and storytelling and performs for all kinds of community groups. In this work, she sees herself as a teacher as well as an entertainer. The activity is still "unfolding" for her, like the title of one of her performances, "Beyond Your Wildest Dreams." It is her hope that she will help her audiences to "share in the unfolding of [her] own dream of bringing peace to the world."

June BORN MAY 11

INTERVIEWED AND PHOTOGRAPHED JULY 19, 2000

June was the fourth child and only girl born in a family of five children. She made her first appearance in a "leaky shack" with a doctor present, in Nebraska, in the foothills of the Rockies. Growing up surrounded by boys and men in a male-dominated part of the country had a lasting effect on her. So did the times into which she was born: "This was during the Depression, Prohibition, no birth control, no telephone in our home, no indoor plumbing, or television."

June was very aware of World War II. Two of her three older brothers were in the service (the third had been blinded as a young child). Around home, she and others were "plane spotters," running out to identify planes flying over. They knew they were near a likely target of enemy planes because Scottsbluff Air Force Base was just a few miles away.

June also remembers rolling cigarettes for her parents since packaged ones were often unavailable. When they did come into the store, June, twelve or thirteen years old at the time, occasionally went to buy them for her parents. She, however, never smoked because her father didn't want her to. "Revering" him, she obeyed.

June owned a stallion and had to ride him four miles every night to give him exercise. She could see him in the pasture from the school assembly. One day she saw him leap over the electrified fence and told the teacher she had to go get him. Another time he was found eating grass in front of the school building and she was called to the superintendent's office. Since she lived close by, it didn't take her long to take her horse home.

June was a "bookworm" and the salutatorian of her high school graduating class. There were no sports for girls, but she liked journalism and worked on the newspaper and yearbook. She was yearbook editor one year. She also worked, mostly babysitting. Influenced by one of her baby-sitting employers, a doctor, June hoped to study medicine. She liked challenges. A case in point: her blind brother wanted to graduate from the public high school, not from a school for the blind. One of June's older brothers tutored him for the oral exams the school agreed to give him and, when that older brother graduated, June continued her blind brother's tutoring. The outcome was successful.

June received a scholarship to a junior college eleven miles from home

but had to earn her room and board in order to stay there. After a year, she was overwhelmed by the demands of work in addition to school, and she decided to leave and find a job. By chance, she passed an Air Force recruiting office and joined up.

Too young to serve overseas, June became a payroll clerk and saw training and service in Texas, Wyoming, New York, and Colorado. At her request, she was transferred to Colorado in place of her best friend, who wanted to stay in Long Island with the man with whom she had fallen in love. In Colorado, at age twenty, June met her present husband, got married, and soon became pregnant.

Shortly after, they both left the service and moved to his Iowa hometown. Her parents had expected her to come back and live near them since her brothers were scattered by then. Her father said to June, "Well, if it doesn't work out . . ." It did work out and Iowa became their ultimate home. But first they spent two years in California, where her husband went to school on the G.I. Bill to learn aircraft mechanics and then worked at an aircraft plant. Their second child was born there.

Back in Iowa, a third child completed the family. June always worked. When the children were small, she worked as a night janitor in a shopping mall. The attractions of the job were the hours, the fact that she could be with the children during the day, and the big discounts she got at the toy store. After that, June was the first female school bus driver in Cedar Rapids, Iowa. She then worked for almost twenty-five years in the office of a wholesale grocery supplier. She liked that job because there was "something to learn."

She worked longer than she anticipated because her husband wanted to buy a used-car business after working for over thirty-three years at Collins Radio, a large electronics company. June now helps out with the car lot, which is next door to their house on the pastoral north side of Cedar Rapids.

She likes cars and maintains a '69 Skylark and an '89 Buick Riviera. Her grown children all live in Iowa, two of them teachers and one a post office employee and coach.

June's view is that women of her age are interested in education and in keeping their families together. She thinks it wrong for single mothers to "advertise" their children born out of wedlock in newspaper birth announcements. When I asked what the women's movement meant to her, she said she is against abortion but all for a woman president. "Onward and upward!" she said.

Marlene BORN MAY 18

INTERVIEWED AND PHOTOGRAPHED JULY 26, 2000

On the day we met, which was punctuated by summer showers, the tuberous begonias and other colorful flowers Marlene has planted in front of her tidy retirement unit were a vivid contrast to the gray day. She was patient as I unloaded my equipment and brought it inside, trying to skirt the rain.

Marlene's most prominent childhood memories are of being very poor and of her mother dying a few months after childbirth, when Marlene was twelve. Marlene was born at home, fourth in a family of nine, in Hills, Iowa. Hunting, fishing, and gardening supplied the family with food. She remembers that it was hard to keep warm in winter and that her brothers had to scrounge for coal. Despite hardships, Marlene says that they managed all right and loved each other.

The children all went to a Catholic school in their town, and later to the Catholic high school in a larger city nearby, their tuition paid for by the diocese. They paid a local boy fifty cents a week to drive them from Hills to school in Iowa City. High school did not require uniforms, and Marlene remembers not having "decent" clothes to wear. Despite that, she had lots of friends in high school. At first, she had to go home after school to help out, but later she was able to stay and attend school sports events. She remarked that it was "different" to go to her friends' homes "where there was a mother."

After high school, there was no money to go to beauty school, as Marlene would have liked. She started work at a soda fountain, then got a better job as a bookkeeper for a local feed company. Marlene married at age nineteen and had one child three years later. She stopped working when her son was born. The family then moved to a farm, where Marlene raised tomatoes to sell to restaurants. An acute illness followed by surgery affected her vision and limited her working activity for a few years. In the 1960s, she and her husband joined her father-in-law in running a large farm market. Some years later, they bought out the farm and the market, which Marlene operated for seventeen more years.

Marlene always liked books but never had any at home and can't remember ever going to a library as a child. She grew up reading *True Romances*. For over ten years, she has worked as an aide at the community library, now com-

bined with the local school library. She does most of the ordering of adult fiction, including large print and audio books. Her pride in the library was shown by the tee shirt she wore for our meeting, which displayed a dinosaur and library slogan.

When she was fourteen or fifteen, Marlene started to smoke and continued until one day in 1994, when she was out of cigarettes for her morning coffee. She decided to quit right then. Her husband, who had stopped earlier, didn't even notice. Two years later she was diagnosed with emphysema and is now dependent on an inhaler.

A widow since 1997, Marlene lives alone in Lone Tree, not far from Hills, the town where she was born and grew up. Her only son lives in town, seriously ill and unable to work. Even now, her surviving brothers and sister would "drop everything" to come and help each other out. Marlene still sees her best friend from high school and has gotten together with classmates annually since 1998. When you grow up and live in a small town, "everyone looks after you in some ways." That has meant the most to her in her life.

As I was leaving, Marlene asked me, "Did I do okay?"

Nancy BORN MAY 19

INTERVIEWED AND PHOTOGRAPHED JULY 28, 2000

Nancy remembers her first six years on a rented farm in southern Michigan as possessing a "lyric beauty." She was alone with her dog and her imagination, and nurtured by her father. Her father, a laborer and a "genius at horse trading"—literally, horse trading—was one of nineteen children and had only a third-grade education. He advised her when she was a "supercilious teen" not to look down on poor people because "they can't help it." Her mother was "fragile" and suffered from migraines. Her two older sisters were a "closed corporation" to her; she was "never scared except alone with them." When Nancy was about ten, her maternal grandmother moved nearby. It became a tradition for Nancy to spend Saturday nights with her, drinking green tea, reading the Bible, and sleeping in an iron bedstead.

In her first elementary school, Nancy felt keenly the differences between rich and poor kids and noted how the teachers "blatantly fawned on rich kids." After the family moved to a better neighborhood, she remembers being treated better. Or was it her IQ test? Or her perfect grades? In high school, Nancy was active in the Honor Society, on the yearbook staff, in art club, piano, and choir, and she wrote the Junior Follies. She reminded some of her teachers of themselves at her age, and they believed it would be a tragedy if she didn't go to college. Bored in school at sixteen, she dreamed of going to the University of Chicago.

Her mother promised Nancy that she could attend college with money left by her grandmother, who had died when Nancy was fourteen, but when the time came, the money was already gone. Nancy worked in a concession stand in a theater and in a factory to earn her first year's tuition and expenses at Chicago. She attended for one wonderful year and hoped to be able to work enough to continue, but getting jobs proved difficult and Nancy's mother said she didn't know what she would do without her at home. Nancy didn't return to college.

Out of Nancy's early experiences came these reflections:

Being born in 1931 meant being sensitized and radicalized by the early and continued perception of inequity and need. I chose (pompously, as befits an intellectual fifteen-year-old) to prefer stray dogs and the disenfranchised . . . to the unaware, smug mainstreamers. I still do prefer them.

She was also watching the world outside.

Being a child of 1931 . . . meant entering adolescence at a time when the world had turned ugly, having one's perceptions forever changed by photographs of bodies stacked like firewood . . . and a mushroom cloud that darkened the sun forever.

Her parents had bought a farm when she graduated from high school, and Nancy lived there with her parents for seventeen more years, developing a growing friendship with both of them. She saw her mother becoming a "different person," enjoying country living, raising chickens, and tending a huge garden. Nancy worked at a series of office jobs, was a rehearsal pianist for a ballet company, and wrote commercials for a TV station. It was at the station that she met her future husband, a photographer.

Married, they moved to Cedar Rapids, Iowa. Nancy had a clerical job at a local hospital for twenty years, first on the graveyard shift, then on rotating shifts. She recalls sleeping in twenty-minute snatches to be able to take her daughter, her only child, to a heady mix of activities during summer vacations.

In the early 1970s, the National Organization of Women (NOW) came to Cedar Rapids. Nancy had been very busy, organizing a Montessori school with some other parents. She attended the first few meetings of NOW but was eventually dismayed at what she saw as the lack of focus on "the real, sole, genuine issue . . . [of] economic equality, starting with equal education." Although she left what she described as a "toxic little group," the experience revealed unpleasant truths about her marriage: her husband had supported her work for the Montessori school but was hostile to time spent on the "lib group" for herself and other women.

Widowed for more than fifteen years after a marriage she regards as always unhappy, Nancy is working still, doing phone survey research. When asked how she, at twenty, would have viewed her present life and self, she said that she still feels twenty inside. And what would her life have been like if she had been born ten years later? She would have been in the right place for herself, emotionally and intellectually; she has always been at least ten years ahead.

When I described the photo Nancy lent me of herself at seventeen as a "glamour shot," she responded sharply with her own reading of the "campy" photograph of "a wild coltish creature," her "feet almost levitating themselves out of loafers."

> My hooves were full of capers. I see — yes, I see! — an innocent put-on of glamour. I see insouciance, hubris, a girl whose sharp mind and fine young body could barely hold themselves within gravity's grasp. I see — yes! — who I still am . . .

Nancy, who writes to me on her 1949 Smith Corona typewriter, claims that, "after years of activity driven by the need for economic survival and adequate parenting, my absolute favorite activity nowadays is not doing anything whatsoever."

Except, of course, caring for her dogs, reading, and expressing her rage poetically: "What was it we had [at seventeen], we females who hadn't been broke to harness? A wildness, a freedom? I want it back."

Susie Anna BORN MAY 25

INTERVIEWED FEBRUARY 13, 2001 PHOTOGRAPHED APRIL 30, 2001

Susie Anna and her husband come every two weeks to spend the afternoon cleaning my house. Susie Anna and I have exchanged stories about our grandchildren, but I knew little about her life until it came out that she and I were both born in 1931. I was aware that she was Mennonite from her tales about fund-raising events for the church and from the little net cap she wears over her bun. We sat down one day to talk before she got to work, and I visited her a couple of months later at her home to photograph her on her back porch.

Susie Anna was born, the fifth of six children, into an Amish family in Kalona, Iowa. The question of how strictly to continue following Amish traditions was central throughout her youth. There were many gradations of traditionalism. Her own parents were "in transition." They joined an Amish Mennonite church, drove cars—but only black ones—and dressed much like the Amish. Her maternal grandparents in Indiana attended a Conservative Mennonite church that permitted cars, but her paternal grandfather, a minister and bishop, was Amish and drove only buggies. Susie Anna met her husband at church youth activities. He and his brother went to a Mennonite Bible school and eventually joined a Conservative Mennonite church. Susie Anna joined the same church even before they married. Her parents would have liked her to go to their church, but there was no rift. Susie Anna says that the line between Amish and Mennonite is more strictly drawn now than it was then.

Her parents farmed, and her father was also a "looked-to" carpenter. That is, people came to him to build barns, houses, sheds, and kitchens. The children helped their mother with the milking. One of the cows was a "kicker," and Father milked her. Susie Anna's father and uncle sawed chunks of ice from a pond in winter and hauled them up a steep hill to an ice house in a shaded area. The ice was stored in layers on the dirt floor of the ice house, with sawdust in between, and was used to supply the homes' ice boxes.

Susie Anna attended a one-room school from kindergarten through eighth grade. There was one teacher, but high turnover. Susie Anna recalls six teachers in nine years. Two of them were men. Discipline in school used to include spanking but, in her time, it consisted of being sent to a small

room downstairs to "talk over problems." Susie Anna's lack of attention once earned her that punishment.

Like most Amish at that time, she did not go to high school. Had Susie Anna been born ten years later, she reflected that she would have likely gone to high school, perhaps even to college. Of her seven children, all have graduated from high school and all but her eldest, who farms the family land, have graduated from college as well.

Susie Anna's oldest brother was drafted in World War II and served as a conscientious objector. Her two older sisters were married during the war, and she recalls that her mother had saved enough packages of Jell-O, rationed like most food, to make Jell-O salad for two hundred people at the wedding receptions.

Susie Anna went to spend time with one of her brothers at a mission outpost in Minnesota when she was about eighteen, and she remembers this, as well as once going to a Bible institute in Ohio, as significant in her life — "getting away from home." She married at twenty-four. The wedding was delayed while her husband-to-be served as a mission-related volunteer in Germany, working with postwar refugees.

After marriage, she was busy with babies and as a farm wife with dairy cows, sheep, hogs, and a big vegetable garden. The five boys and two girls were born between 1956 and 1971. Susie Anna and her husband were engaged in many church-related volunteer activities — Sunday evening socials for church youth, helping at summer Bible school, serving on church committees as trustees, and helping clean the church.

When she was over fifty, Susie Anna started to work outside her home, cleaning other people's houses. It began when a woman from church wanted to give up some of her cleaning jobs, and Susie Anna took over. The work is mostly in Iowa City, some twenty miles from Kalona, and she is busy four days a week, with two jobs on some days. In 1990 her husband had a heart attack and had to give up his job at a feed store because it involved heavy hauling. Since then, they have worked together at her jobs. They are still working, with time off for trips to see the children who live in other states, and for extended family reunions. They have twelve grandchildren.

Leah BORN MAY 31

INTERVIEWED JUNE 2001 PHOTOGRAPHED OCTOBER 16, 2001

Leah answered the interview questions by e-mail over a period of a couple of weeks from London, where she has lived for sixteen years. That doesn't necessarily give her the *last* word, but it does give me very *many* of her words. This is appropriate enough since she has long been a writer and is now a poet. She wrote about being born in 1931:

> Two years before, a tower of ticker tape came crashing down, and two years later Hitler came to power. In between, the tallest building seen on earth first pierced the sky, and I was born. *Where* is as significant as *when* . . . Often I wonder why life has been so kind to me, so cruel to others . . .

The last sentence reflects Leah's compassion, which led her into the life of an activist in the 1960s and 1970s, but she attributes much of what she did to "a great measure of luck." She says that she "fell into" the movements.

> The dangerous milk [containing Strontium 90 from atomic tests] led me to Women Strike for Peace, which in turn led me to think more deeply about the world and politics, and to become something of an activist. In turn, that led me to write for publication, since I felt I had important things to say. I fell into the civil rights movement because of racist attitudes in New York regarding schoolchildren that shocked me when my own children were entering school. And I was introduced to feminism at a Women Strike for Peace rally in Washington in 1967.

Leah was born in New York, the second of two girls whose parents had both emigrated from Eastern Europe as children. Her father was an architect. The family moved to Brooklyn when Leah was very young and stayed there until she was in kindergarten, the move dictated by the Depression.

Leah remembers churning butter in school as part of a Thanksgiving celebration, wearing crepe paper Pilgrim costumes, and looking "cute." When they came back to New York, Leah attended, first, a good, progressive public school in a well-to-do neighborhood. Then her parents bought a house so that her father could have an office at home. It was on a "borderline" street in a poor neighborhood. The school was "in every way deprived." Leah's parents managed to have Leah transferred back to the good school, but she

says, "The fact that poor children had got a bad deal in the public school system was not lost on me, and greatly affected my political attitudes for the rest of my life."

Leah was accepted at Hunter College High School but transferred to a small private coed day school after two years of failing some courses and making them up in summer school. She grants that the teaching at Hunter was mostly very good, and she has never forgotten how the geometry teacher smiled to herself after writing a theorem on the blackboard, saying to the class, "That's beautiful." But she resented the six to eight hours of homework. She already knew that she wanted to be a writer and did a lot of reading and writing on her own. Outside of school, Leah lived a "New York life," going with friends to museums, foreign films, parties and, later, nightclubs.

There were many refugee children in her elementary school and in the summer camps she attended. In her bunk at camp were several girls from Belgium who woke up screaming with nightmares. President Roosevelt's death greatly upset her and her parents. He had seemed a "father figure." She also remembers crying with her father over the dropping of the first atom bomb.

Leah went to Syracuse University in upstate New York. Preferring to spend her time working on the student newspaper, Leah cut classes and left Syracuse after one term. She returned to the city, worked at a number of clerical and secretarial jobs, even "ghost writing for a sleazy literary agency," and volunteered at a hospital. She married when she was twenty-four and continued to work for a couple of years. Then it was financially possible to stay at home and write when the spirit moved her. She liked that: "Although I'm a serious feminist, I never thought that working at some boring job was a requirement." She is a night person and thinks of herself as lazy.

Leah gave birth to two daughters when she was in her twenties, and soon she was working for the social issues that concerned her. Among other activities, Leah wrote for a newsletter published by Harlem parents about schools and for one year served as administrator for a tutoring program in Harlem. She had help with the children from her parents, who lived in an apartment in the same building, and from her husband "who always pitched in." Leah "usually wrote late at night when the children were asleep." Her writing began to appear in publications in 1967. She studied short-story writing in night classes at Columbia University for two and a half years.

In the 1970s, Leah got to know some of the big names in the women's movement, including Andrea Dworkin, Robin Morgan, Barbara Deming, and others, who became friends and, she says, "taught me a thing or two." In 1979 Beacon Press published Leah's book *Dreamers & Dealers: An Intimate Appraisal of the Women's Movement*. It is dedicated to her mother.

When Leah reflects on the women's movement now, she says that its most important contributions to her life have been "the concept of sisterhood and an increased sense of my own dignity." She believes that the political gains have been slight and are always imperiled but that "to some extent, we have forced men to listen, to give lip service to equality and to recognize our latent power . . ." She is more aware now of the effect of socioeconomic differences on the lives of women, the advantages that relatively affluent middle-class women have over their poorer sisters. She cautions against intolerance of women toward each other and says, "Chew the slogans over before you swallow them. The women's movement that I was once active in has infiltrated my being and I trust it to lead me where I ought to go. I no longer march."

Leah's husband was able to retire early from an executive career in printing production, and they relocated to London. He has always painted, and that is his main occupation now. I can attest to a studio in their apartment filled with large canvases depicting dreamlike juxtapositions of ordinary and unusual subjects. Leah writes of her choice of mate, "How I made such a wise decision at such a stupid age still confounds me." He was present during our photo shoot and indeed, photographed me photographing her.

Leah has concentrated on poetry since the move and has published three slim volumes, *From Cookie to Witch Is an Old Story*, *Somewhere en Route: Poems 1987–1992*, and *The Way to Go* (Bristol: Loxwood Stoneleigh). She gives poetry readings and attends many given by other poets; she is part of the London poetry scene. Leah feels that the British culture in which she now lives has made her less outspoken, "more circumspect." As she says, "I do now try to think before blurting things out, and that may be why my poetry . . . now is in formal verse. Considerations of form force one to stop and think."

One grown daughter now lives in New York, the other, a photographer, lives in Turkey and has just had her second child. Leah says she has become more like her mother as she has grown older: "I worry about my children who live far away. I worry in detail." One thing hasn't changed. Leah began smoking at fifteen, secretly, and is still a heavy smoker. It seems to go together with writing.

Leah and I exchanged many e-mails beyond the interview questions and answers, several of them about poetry. As a lapsed poet but still a reader of poetry, I was interested in her poems and in what she liked in contemporary poetry. After our photography session, we left her husband and their dog, Flake, and she took me to the Poetry Library in Festival Hall on the south bank of the Thames and to look in on a café called the Poetry Place, where poets gather and readings are held. Her contentment with her transplanted life is expressed in the title poem of her most recent volume, *The Way to Go*:

> . . . sounds of drilling in the street, a cat
> idling in the dooryard, knocking over
> the neighbour's dustbin. So you'd never guess
> that these late years I've mainly lived in clover.

In "Long Distance," from the same volume and addressed to one of her daughters, the poet muses,

> . . . we both have travelled far
> and you are safe — and home is anywhere.

Ethel BORN JUNE 4

INTERVIEWED DECEMBER 19, 2000 PHOTOGRAPHED MARCH 26, 2001

When Ethel contacted me about the project by e-mail, she wanted to know the point of it, but she already knew a lot, from a New Yorker's point of view:

> . . . 1931 was the year the George Washington Bridge was opened and the Empire State Building went up. On the other hand, I think it had the lowest birth rate in history and was the very worst year of the Great Depression. Is the latter what interests you?

Ethel has lived in the same East Side Manhattan neighborhood since she was eight. Her parents immigrated from Norway as young people; her grandparents remained there. She was taken to Norway as an infant for a year, and her first language was Norwegian. In New York, she remembers her father not wanting them to speak Norwegian in public. He was a handyman and, for a time, the family lived in a church where he was sexton and caretaker. Ethel wrote about the effects of the Depression on her parents.

> [They] were indelibly stamped with the fear of a repetition of those years of insecurity [and] deprivation . . . I don't think anyone ever gets over praying for snow so that you can take your new snow shovel door-to-door with an offer to clear the sidewalk.

An only child in her immediate family and wider environment, Ethel received more than her share of attention and gifts. This "peculiar combination" of attention and insecurity made her a person with "an overdeveloped sense of responsibility." As she says, "The only child has to be both son and daughter, wage earner and nurturer, defender and caregiver."

At the same time, "Papa's bank account"—not Mama's, as in the book of that name—gave her a feeling of security, as did her feeling that "if worse came to worst, the city would take care of me . . . I once had great faith in New York City."

Ethel skipped a grade in elementary school because she had impressed a teacher who liked to use foreign phrases and noticed Ethel copying them down. Selected to be in the elite Country School of Julia Richman High School, Ethel found it "one long push." She was encouraged when her homeroom teacher told her parents, "I wouldn't let one of my girls get thrown out of Country School." Ethel was active with the literary magazine. She also

played the role of a princess from an un-specified Balkan country in a school pro-duction, with an accent many classmates took to be genuine.

Her perception is that the large majority of girls in her classes were Jewish and from West Side professional families. She recalls their cashmere sweaters, lockets, and loafers scrunched down in back for better shuffling. She thinks most of the non-Jewish girls were from working-class families. Their cheaper loafers were too stiff to scrunch down.

Ethel went on to Queens College, one of the colleges of the New York City system. The commute involved three subways and a bus ride. From a very early age, she had put any gifts of money in the bank for college. It never occurred to her to take a commercial track in high school or not to go to college. She loved Queens College. Her classes were less than half the size of those in her high school, and it was coed. She took a split major in speech and English and minored in philosophy. Men could major in "impractical" subjects and then go on to law school to be able to get good jobs. Women "didn't have an awful lot of choices." Her high school didn't permit college-bound students to take typing, which would at least have prepared them for the jobs they were likely to get.

A teacher at Queens advised Ethel to approach the television networks for a position as a production assistant and suggested she mention his name. She did and got a job . . . as a receptionist. Ethel has worked at a succession of proofreading and editing jobs for newspapers and trade publications, in-cluding a ten-year stint as marketing and merchandising editor of a trade magazine. She then became a freelancer and still does some freelance proof-reading. Ethel notes that the editors were all men and women were the assis-tant editors. Harassment was commonplace. In every job she had, she was "chased around the desk." She saw times changing, however. A contribution

of the women's movement, small but important, was influencing the *New York Times* to stop segregating help-wanted ads by "male" or "female."

Ethel never married, although she had expected marriage to be part of her life. Ethel saw her mother as the "peacemaker" in the family, but she "didn't want to be [her] mother" because her father "made the rules." In marriage, she learned early, the man was the boss because he held the purse strings.

Ethel assumes that women of her age probably share her experiences of harassment on the job and difficulty in getting jobs, especially good jobs. She would like to have been a boomer, born in 1948. In 1968 she would have been twenty and, she fantasizes, she could have gone to the Democratic National Convention in Chicago as a student at Northwestern University.

Ethel started smoking at Queens College, encouraged by the ashtrays on every table, and didn't stop until she was diagnosed with emphysema in 1990. She is actively engaged on the Internet with others suffering from pulmonary disease. Living on the fifth floor of a walk-up brownstone, she gets up the stairs "once a day, and slowly." She is busy managing the paperwork regarding her illness and working, when she can.

The bright yellow walls of her apartment, the books and posters, the wall of family pictures — including a favorite photograph of her father, laughing, and a painting of her, nude, as a young woman — create a distinctive environment. She served me sandwiches and wine, and showed me some of her own black-and-white photography.

Her e-mail address includes the word *maverick*.

Wanda BORN JUNE 5

INTERVIEWED AND PHOTOGRAPHED SEPTEMBER 27, 2000

Before we met, Wanda wrote in an e-mail, "I am not exactly sure what is expected of me. We are just average people with average thoughts and desires." For eight years, with five children, this "average" woman owned and operated Wanda's Café in Brandon, Iowa. This was her daily schedule, except on Thanksgiving, Christmas, and Easter, when the restaurant was closed: she opened at 5 A.M. for breakfast and worked through the noon rush, offering one special plus the "usual," then went upstairs, where the family lived, for a fifteen-minute nap and to do chores, then returned at 5 P.M. to serve short orders and to clean up, closing at 10 P.M.

Wanda was born on a farm in Cedar County, Iowa, the middle one of three children. Her parents were able to save the farm through the Depression by their "wise spending" and frugality. The family went to town once a week to sell eggs. Wanda's paternal grandparents had retired from farming and moved to town, and on these weekly trips, the children used to buy a nickel's worth of candy and walk to their grandparents' house. Wanda remembers sitting on the front porch and sharing the candy with her grandmother, who was "sweet and loving."

Wanda's parents came from very different backgrounds, which they used to complement each other in their marriage. Her mother and her mother's siblings all attended Cornell College in Mount Vernon, Iowa, but her father left school after the eighth grade. He was imaginative, always inventing things, and her mother, who had studied chemistry and math, could help him figure out how to construct what he had in mind. She had arthritis and he built several different elevators for her in their home.

Wanda went to a one-room elementary school one-half mile from home, walking over snowbanks in winter to get there. For high school, she went to Tipton, a nearby town, which she remembers as an exciting change. She loved school, was outgoing, and went out for acting and music. She made friends easily and has kept up with some of them to this day. Her memories of the war focus on rationing of sugar and shoes. Mother canned fruit, so there wasn't much sugar left for other purposes. Wanda was good at jumping rope, but that meant she was hard on shoes. After high school, she wanted to get out and get a job. She was a good typist and was hired by a tractor dealership in Cedar Rapids. She wasn't on her own for long.

At eighteen, Wanda married a farmer she met at a Junior Farm Bureau party, and she had five children in the next nine years. When her youngest started school, Wanda began restaurant work on a 5 A.M. to 2 P.M. shift so she could be home when the children returned from school. Experience in a couple of other restaurant jobs and the encouragement of patrons led her to open Wanda's Café. Running the restaurant gave her a new sense of self-esteem. When state health and safety requirements would have been too costly to implement, she closed the restaurant. Reflecting now, she wrote, "I have lots of wonderful memories from the restaurant times but it was a lot of hard work too. But as the years have gone by I know that hard work never hurt me—it just made me a stronger individual."

Wanda's life began to be oriented toward Vinton, Iowa, a town of five thousand. She worked at a JC Penney, a lumberyard, and then for the city of Vinton for sixteen years, until her retirement in 1993. While working for the city, Wanda and the three other office staff joined in protest after several years of raises being given to all city employees except office staff . . . the only women employees. They contacted the Teamsters Union and proceeded to unionize their office. The atmosphere was "unpleasant," Wanda wrote, "but it paid off. From then on we got the same raises . . . as all the others . . . I normally don't go out looking for trouble but that time I really thought it was necessary."

Meanwhile, her husband's escalating debts were affecting Wanda's health and state of mind. With her father's financial help, she bought a house in Vinton, where she still lives, and divorced her husband after thirty-four years of marriage. She remarried, happily, a few years later. In her youth, she said, she would never have expected either divorcing or remarrying. Also unexpected is that she and her husband are now on friendly terms with her first husband and his wife: "We have let the past become the past and have learned to go on in the future." It is "much easier for the children too."

Wanda is an active volunteer in several programs, both in Vinton and in Sun City, Arizona, where she spends four winter months. She is also a quilter with an attic sewing room filled with materials and projects in process. She never sells her quilts, choosing instead to give them away, mostly to family. She plays the piano at church and is teaching someone to play. Health conscious, she walks regularly and tries to eat carefully. She participates in a lipid research project at the teaching hospital of the University of Iowa. She says that she makes good pies and they are her great temptation.

After our work together was over, Wanda served lunch and then directed me on a drive around the town of Vinton to point out recent improvements: new streetlights, refurbished buildings, murals on some outside walls. She didn't want to be driven home: she said she would walk as part of her exercise for the day.

Dorothy BORN JUNE 7

INTERVIEWED AND PHOTOGRAPHED JULY 17, 2000

Although Dorothy was born and grew up in Chicago, she has lived in the small town of Mount Vernon, Iowa, for most of her life. She was curious about the project and about me, and we discovered that we had both married after two years of college. Dorothy was only the second woman I met, and I thought it quite natural to find this echo of my life in hers. As I met more of the women, I continued to find echoes, but I learned not to expect them.

Dorothy's high school in a far-south suburb of Chicago was racially integrated because the neighborhood was, although housing wasn't. She always had African American friends. She remembers major racial disturbances in the city in the postwar years.

"Shy, fairly popular, and studious" in high school, Dorothy first went to Mount Vernon to go to Cornell College. She left college to marry when she was twenty, confirming her parents' expectations that girls receive two years of college education while boys—including her brother—receive four. She now realizes that she was conforming to society's expectations as well. She had two sons, born when she was in her late twenties, and when her younger went to kindergarten, Dorothy returned to complete her degree in biology on a part-time basis. She recalls bursting into tears at graduation when asked what she now expected to do.

In the mid-1970s, Dorothy began to work in the college admissions office to provide for her boys' college education. Later she worked at another college in the area, concurrently earning the master's degree required for her position in the Office of Continuing Education. Looking back, she reflects that all the work she has done is tied to the problem solving she learned when studying biology.

In the mid-1980s, Dorothy divorced her husband and moved far from the area for a position at Virginia Wesleyan College. She worked there for twelve years, retiring at sixty-five and moving back to Chicago to join her former sister-in-law in a new business. She encountered her former husband again, and they soon remarried. Dorothy believes that the divorce and her years of independent work gave her the chance she needed to grow as a person. Had she been a young woman in the 1960s, instead of in the 1950s, she thinks she would have pursued her "adventures" earlier in her life. She re-

married the same man because the durable basis of their marriage emerged when they met again.

Now they are Red Cross disaster volunteers, traveling to areas of need, spending about four months a year on this cause. When I spoke to her recently, they had just returned from four weeks helping out in flooded communities along the Mississippi. It was their tenth stint. They also travel for adventure at least once a year, to places such as Antarctica and the Amazon.

About the influence of her year of birth, Dorothy wrote,

Growing up in the Depression years influenced many aspects of my personality, values and day-to-day habits . . . [T]he ability to have and hold a job, to work hard so you don't lose a job were extremely important. I can remember how proud my Dad was as he told people that he never lost his job . . .

I also grew up at a time . . . when one's goal as a teenager was to marry and have children. These expectations were often in conflict with a need to discover and reach my potential. Consequently, the women's movement was very meaningful to me.

. . . [G]rowing up in the 30s and 40s helped me to value the importance of people rather than material things. The concern for one's neighbors and their welfare . . . became a vital part of my personality as shown by my commitment to volunteerism.

The very best contribution of the 30s to my life . . . was a result of no television and no computers. I grew up surrounded by books and my happiest childhood memories involve the world of books.

Catherine BORN JUNE 13

INTERVIEWED AND PHOTOGRAPHED JANUARY 19, 2002

One of Catherine's twin sons refers to the "'31 Club," consisting of Catherine, Althea, and some of their friends. This clubbiness, which the women endorse, expresses their upbeat attitude toward their age. At seventy, Catherine says she has had "a good, privileged life" and that she is proud of her good health. She never would have imagined how much she and her husband would be traveling—and enjoying it.

Catherine was born in a college town, Petersburg, Virginia, at home, the last of seven children. It was a close family, a musical family, a family bent on education. All but one sister are still living. Catherine's mother taught before marriage. As a married woman, she couldn't teach, but there were children to take care of at home. Catherine's father was a janitor. Catherine says he was "very bright" but had not had the opportunity for schooling. Her mother was a college graduate but didn't have enough challenges after raising her children. This is why Catherine and her husband believe they must "keep going as much as possible."

Catherine started school when she was five. Her mother was ready, she says, not to have children at home any longer. Catherine attended a large, all-Black six-grade school used by Virginia State College for its student teachers. Catherine loved school, brought a peanut butter and jelly sandwich, and stayed all day. For seventh grade through high school, the school was farther from home. Her older siblings had no transportation provided and had to pass three white schools on the way to theirs, but a teacher arranged for a bus to bring Catherine and her classmates to school. They had to walk home or take a city bus back.

Virginia only required eleven years of schooling at that time, although Catherine isn't sure whether that minimum requirement was statewide. She was in the top classes and "loved to talk." Talking got her in trouble with a math teacher, who "told on her" to her mother and failed her the first quarter. This tattling disturbed Catherine because the teacher's family and hers were close. She managed to bring her math grade up to 90 in the next marking period.

There was always a piano in the house, and Catherine started lessons when she was around eight years old. Her second teacher, whom she knew from church, was on the faculty of the local college. In high school, Catherine

sang in choral groups. She doesn't recall many other extracurricular activities. After graduation, she went to Virginia State, as all her brothers and sisters had. The two sisters closest to her in age had only completed two years, and her parents were determined that she would last the whole four. Catherine had always wanted to be a teacher and, since high school, a music teacher. She majored in music education and sang in the choir. The choir was required to sing at Sunday chapel services so, as she puts it, she worked seven days a week.

Two of her brothers and her sister who worked in New York came home for Catherine's college graduation and, as planned, she was "all packed and ready to go back with them." Her oldest brother convinced their father to let her go, although Father thought it was time she started to work. As her husband retells this story he has heard from her, she "left before the ink was dry on her diploma." She went to New York to study for a master's degree at New York University, as her two older brothers had done. When I asked how she happened to choose a private university over a city one, thinking of the costs, she told me that the state of Virginia paid the out-of-state tuition because they would not accept Black students at the University of Virginia! Catherine lived with her oldest brother in the Bronx, worked mornings in a department store in Brooklyn, and attended classes starting at 4 P.M. on the lower Manhattan campus. (Non–New Yorkers should be aware that this is a lot of travel.)

Coming to New York, following in her siblings' footsteps, and knowing that she wanted to teach music there, Catherine says that she was nevertheless "naïve." At home she had been sheltered and had never thought about race. It was in New York that she learned about race from the accumulation of acts that she came to perceive as racist. She did not care to elaborate.

After graduation, Catherine was licensed to teach grades seven through twelve. After a brief placement in a Brooklyn school, she taught general music and chorus in the Bronx for two years. When her brother, with whom she still lived, moved to Queens, Catherine bought her first car and he taught her to drive. In 1956 a new school opened in Queens for grades seven through nine, with places for two music teachers. Catherine taught there with a fellow student from NYU for eight years, leaving only when pregnant. The year before, through a friend, she had met a man who was looking for a bridge partner. Catherine was only learning bridge, but she was interested in "finding a mate." They married. They now play in bridge tournaments, so both must have found the right partner.

Two years after her daughter was born, Catherine was pregnant again and "surprised" to give birth to twin boys. Her father-in-law had predicted that she was carrying twins but, unfortunately, he died two weeks to the day before he would have been proven correct. Catherine stayed home for ten years with the children, then taught in a Queens school with a specialized music program until she retired in 1990. She also taught choral singing, and her pupils performed in school assemblies and at least twice a year in other venues outside of school, often as fund-raisers for school.

Catherine has always belonged to outside choral groups as well as singing in church. She thinks she might have developed her own talents more if she had had specialized training. As it is, she enjoys singing, as she enjoys life.

Jeannette BORN JUNE 19

INTERVIEWED AND PHOTOGRAPHED APRIL 23, 2001

Jeannette had two older sisters, the younger only a year older than she. In her Catholic elementary school in Dubuque, Iowa, it seemed that teachers were always comparing her to her sister. Once, in second grade, Jeannette stood up and declared that she was *not* her sister, she was herself. After school that day, her teacher and another nun walked her home to tell her mother. Her mother believed that "authority was always right," but Jeannette does not remember a significant punishment for her declaration of independence. She was undeterred.

When she was eight, Jeannette came home for lunch to find that her mother was in the hospital having a baby. There were already two children younger than she in the family. Jeannette had not been told this was going to happen and felt insulted. In fact, she was "livid" and did not want to return to school that day. Grandmother, her mother's mother, who lived with them, persuaded her to return. Jeannette now reflects that things like pregnancy and sex were never talked about at home.

In fifth grade, Jeannette encountered a very understanding teacher who had not had her older sisters in class. They often sat and talked, and Jeannette remembers carrying Sister Laurentia's books and walking her back to the convent. Sister Laurentia told her, "You can do whatever you want to do."

Jeannette was active in musical activities in high school. She played the violin and was in several singing groups. One of her earliest memories is of her paternal grandfather making a violin for her fourth birthday, bringing it to her, and dying later the same day. She had friends but not much time for them. She cleaned houses and babysat for her spending money.

Jeannette went to Clark College in Dubuque on a four-year scholarship, one of only three students in her high school class of fifty-nine to go on with their education. Her mother had taught school before she married, and her grandmother had also been a teacher. There was a family expectation that Jeannette would follow that path, but she knew she didn't want to teach. She wanted to be an accountant or, second best, a lawyer. She was told there were no women accountants or lawyers. She chose to become a dietician.

In her junior year, Jeannette met her future husband at a party that she

had reluctantly attended. She was too busy. But he was a good dancer, one thing led to another, and they were married after she graduated in 1953. They had a girl and then two boys between 1955 and 1959. Jeannette's husband served in the Navy for two years and then went back to college to become a nurse anesthetist. Jeannette began her long career as a hospital dietician while he was studying from 1956 to 1958, then she took a ten-year break from work in a hospital to do consulting from home. She resumed working as a consulting dietician in Cedar Falls, Iowa, at the hospital, care centers, and with individuals, limiting her working hours to when the children were in school or her husband was at home. His hours in surgery began very early and he was generally home by noon. They moved to Temple, Texas, and she continued working. As a volunteer, she also helped seniors with tax preparation.

Jeannette's husband, her "best friend," died in 1991, and she had to learn to do things she had never done, such as pumping gas and mowing the lawn. It was a bitter experience to be "disinvited" from a couples group they had belonged to. Two years later, she moved to Iowa City, Iowa, to be near her daughter. She is an active quilter, another expression of her "artistic bent," which had earlier led her to design and sew clothes for the family. She is also busy as a volunteer.

Although Jeannette never wanted "to be labeled the same as anyone else," she is surprised at how well she succeeded in being different: "I never thought I'd really be who I am." People listened to her in her professional role, building her confidence. She has always been willing to speak up, not satisfied that "black is black and white is white."

When she was diagnosed with breast cancer late in 2000, Jeannette started reading to learn about her disease. She underwent three surgeries and two biopsies in six weeks. When she speaks of the disease, it is to express her determination to beat it.

Jeannette says that she grew up enveloped in family activities. It was a life independent of outside stimulation: "We were always active, 'intermingly' with one another. We learned how to entertain ourselves. Imaginations were not idle. I was never bored."

Gaja BORN JUNE 21

INTERVIEWED AND PHOTOGRAPHED MARCH 9, 2001

Gaja came to my hotel room in Singapore for our meeting. When I opened the door for her, she spontaneously embraced me. Dressed in a brilliant emerald green sari with royal blue and gold trim, she was weighed down by a bag of materials to show me: booklets about the Singapore Children's Society, where she has worked for forty-three years; a photo album from her four-month stay in the United States in 1972 with social workers from many countries; documents and photographs from her years of education and training. Although out of breath from her exertions, made worse by her interstitial lung disease, she was more eager to show me and tell me things than to rest.

Gaja was born in Kuala Lumpur, Malaysia, and moved with her family to Singapore when she was two. Gaja had an older and a younger sister, and after a few years, the family included her grandparents and some cousins brought to Singapore for their education. Gaja felt no generation gap, only continuity in this extended family.

Mother had been an "overprotected only child," born sixteen years after her parents' marriage. Tutored at home and herself married at fourteen, she was good in mathematics and tutored the children in math, as well as in the Tamil and English alphabets. She also played music with them. As the girls became older, they read Tamil and English newspapers with their father. Father was a civil servant in the Treasury under the British. In 1942, as the Japanese were about to overwhelm Singapore and the British were preparing to leave, he was not permitted to evacuate. He was required to stay and destroy money and records to keep them out of Japanese hands. The grandparents, Gaja's mother, and the three girls could have left but would not do so without him: "We were prepared to die together."

The war years were hard. All schools and enterprises had to be conducted in Japanese. It was more difficult for Gaja's father to learn this language than for the girls, so they helped him in the evenings. They were always very hungry. In school, the children received a terrible-tasting bread cooked in palm oil and a banana every day to bring home. They couldn't help but eat some on the way. Gaja also remembers queuing for sugar and broken rice, and her mother bartering saris and bangles for food with families who had hoarded supplies.

After the war, Gaja returned for five years to the Raffles Girls' School she had attended before the Japanese came and commandeered the building. Instruction was in English, strictly, and girls were fined for speaking any other language, even out of the classroom. Gaja's older sister had become a teacher, and her father said that teaching was a good career for women, so Gaja entered a "crash program" in teacher training. She discovered that, although she loved children, she found it hard to relate to so many all at once. She also suffered from frequent colds and coughs.

In Singapore in 1950, there were no professionally qualified social workers. So-called almoners from Great Britain helped to train volunteers for the newly founded Singapore Children's Society. They looked for volunteers among graduates of teacher training programs. Gaja began at the Singapore Maternity Hospital as such a volunteer and, with this experience plus an entrance exam, qualified for entrance to a postgraduate course at the University of Malaya in Singapore. She completed the program in 1958 and was the society's employee with the longest tenure as of 2001. The Scotswoman who was head of the Department of Social Studies and Gaja's mentor wrote about her in a letter of reference, "She has a gentle unruffled personality and establishes good relationships with those with whom she works, wherever she goes." Gaja told an interviewer in 1991 that she became involved in social work because "I was influenced by my family members of three generations who were involved in voluntary charitable work . . ."

Gaja is working long past the mandatory retirement age, having received extensions year by year, but she expects to retire at the end of 2001. She plans to tutor mathematics, first as a volunteer and eventually with private pupils, and to return to playing the oboe with an amateur orchestra. Had she been born ten years earlier, Gaja might have been "forced to marry." As it was, her parents were broad-minded. Had she been born ten years later, she might have suffered as a vulnerable baby or small child from the wartime shortages.

Over tea, Gaja and I discovered that we had both signed up to be organ donors and had executed advanced medical directives. She said that she doesn't want a traditional Indian funeral—it is "too traumatic." With one more hug, she left with her heavy bag of treasures, just a little lighter for those she had given me.

Celia BORN JULY 13

INTERVIEWED AND PHOTOGRAPHED NOVEMBER 29, 2000

Celia always wanted to be a nurse, and she fulfilled her ambition. But after all, she asked, what could a girl become? A secretary, a teacher, or a nurse. Her mother was a teacher but, after her marriage, only held a teaching position during World War II since women with families were not hired under usual circumstances.

Celia was the only girl in the family, with two older and two younger brothers. Their father farmed on hilly land in Viola, Iowa, and managed to add acreage during the Depression years although they had little cash. Celia remembers,

> We were poor but lived well by the standards of the 30s. Family life was different, we had chores which were important jobs in the family's daily life such as bringing in wood to heat with . . . water from the pump, caring for the animals, etc.

Celia was left-handed and, when she started school, her mother told the teacher not to try to change her. That was something that was still being done. (My mother also went to school on behalf of my left-handedness.) The school building Celia attended served all twelve grades, and two to three grades were taught in one room. This arrangement sometimes resulted in subjects being taught in an untraditional sequence. For example, Celia remembers studying geometry before algebra. When Celia was in seventh grade, her mother, who was then teaching kindergarten, first, and second grades, was diagnosed with breast cancer. Celia's mother was responsible for hiring her own substitute.

One term in high school, when a physics class had been scheduled, Celia persuaded two other girls that business math would be a better choice. The class was permitted to vote and the result was a tie. The teacher chose physics, revealing he had already ordered the books. In her last two years, there was basketball for girls and Celia played. Her graduating class consisted of herself and one other.

When Celia was still in high school, her mother died. To some extent, the family shared responsibilities—her father made breakfast, and an older brother, back from the service, stayed home about a year before going to the university—but Celia was "chief cook and housecleaner." She was aware

that many women in the community expected her to stay home and take care of things, but her father, who hadn't gone beyond eighth grade himself, wanted her to go on with her education. She enrolled in and graduated from the three-year diploma program in nursing at the University of Iowa. There were more than seventy students starting out in her class, all living in an on-campus dormitory under strict rules.

Celia married when she was twenty-one, after graduation but before taking her State Board exams. She worked as a registered nurse throughout her life until retirement in 1991, except for the years before her two children started school. Her husband's career in education took the family to Buffalo Center, Mason City, Des Moines, and ultimately, Iowa City, Iowa. Celia worked in successively larger hospitals, as well as in a care center. She managed also to be a Camp Fire Girls leader, a Cub Scout assistant leader, and a Sunday school teacher.

In retirement, Celia pursues her interest in sewing as a charter member of the American Sewing Guild. She and her husband provide weekly support for their local grandson's guitar lessons, including transportation. Celia is currently dealing with her own cancer. Our getting together was delayed to allow for trips we both had planned and for treatment she was receiving. When we met, she was not pleased with a recent haircut. It was "too short," and she said her hair had grown in "different."

Living through the Depression made a difference in one's attitude, Celia thinks, and supposes that attitude would characterize other women of her age. It is true that many of the women expressed similar views. Celia has trouble throwing "perfectly good stuff" away, and when she sees young women buying quantities of household furnishings in preparation for marriage, she thinks to herself, "Do you really need all that?"

Hazel BORN JULY 22

INTERVIEWED SEPTEMBER 25, 2000 (RE-)PHOTOGRAPHED OCTOBER 3, 2000

Hazel had warm homemade apple crisp and coffee ready when I arrived. I usually preferred to work before accepting an offer to eat something, but Hazel's hospitality could not be refused. It met a subsequent challenge as well. Something went wrong with the film developing, and I had to return and photograph Hazel again. She graciously dressed up again for a second sitting. Perhaps her willingness had something to do with the envy she reported on the part of some of her siblings that *she* had been chosen for this project.

Hazel is a surviving twin and married to a surviving twin. She and her twin sister were born at home into a family with five children. She finds it amazing that her parents seemed so "relaxed," never hinting at the problem of having twin girls after five others. Her father was a veterinarian in a small central Iowa town, and her mother acted as his receptionist, often telling farmers where he was so they could flag him down. Before Hazel's mother married, she was a seamstress, going to people's homes to work. Although she was forty-four when the girls were born, she was better dressed than the other mothers and was someone to whom other children seemed to gravitate.

Hazel was left-handed and always had trouble with penmanship. Her husband is also a lefty but turns the paper at an angle to write better. Hazel's mother went to school to tell the teacher not to "change" her. (Hazel, Celia, and I share the handedness, the penmanship problem, and the defending mother!)

Hazel's father was a major influence on her. She never smoked because "Father didn't like to see women smoke," although he himself chewed tobacco. When she had the early ambition to become a nurse, her father said he didn't want her "emptying bedpans." He would have liked her to become a teacher, and she went away to Simpson College in Indianola, Iowa, a liberal arts college known for producing teachers. She was very homesick at college and, although her parents moved to Indianola late in her freshman year, she left after one year because she wanted "to get a job and earn money." She thinks her father was probably disappointed in her for leaving. She did become part of the life of a teacher, however, by marrying a former fellow student who went on to become a teacher and, later, a school administrator.

Hazel married at twenty-one, when her husband was a senior at Simpson. He was in the army during the Korean War, and Hazel lived with her parents. When their daughter was born, he saw her at a few weeks old and then only after he returned from Japan eighteen months later. Hazel and her husband moved several times in pursuit of his career in education, always in Iowa, while having and raising another daughter and a son. Their son, born in 1965, was the first baby of the year in their community but somehow missed out on the gifts usually given by the local newspaper.

Hazel and I both have daughters born in 1954. We reminisced about how they were only allowed to wear pants to school in winter after they had started high school. Hazel recalled that the local school's rule was that it had to be zero degrees or colder but that one day she sent the two girls to school in pants because she thought it was "cold enough." Other mothers followed her lead.

After a number of jobs, in banks and elsewhere, Hazel worked twenty-three years as a tax preparer at a law firm. She decided to retire "before they wanted to get rid of me," but the firm called her back and she expects to work at least one more tax season. She loves the work—the numbers, the interviews.

She reads a lot, knits ("but nothing fancy"), and has taken up her husband's love of fishing. His paintings, a postretirement occupation, are proudly hung. She sees "marrying young and staying together" as one of the determinants of her life—that, and her "good parents."

What surprises Hazel about her life now? That she has ended up in such a small town, Oxford Junction, Iowa, and that she is an old woman but doesn't feel like one. But then, her mother, who lived to be eighty-four, once told her that she still felt young "inside."

Alice BORN AUGUST 28

INTERVIEWED JANUARY 15, 2001 PHOTOGRAPHED MARCH 27, 2001

Alice and I were best friends when we were eight years old, but we hadn't seen each other since we were about twelve. We met for me to take photographs of her in the school building that replaced the elementary school we attended on the Upper West Side in New York City, still called P.S. 87. This place seemed appropriate both because it was the scene of our friendship and because Alice's career had been in elementary school teaching. Her daughter Carol was present and photographed our reunion in a large sunny classroom that I obtained permission to use during the lunch period.

Alice's vivid memories of the twice-weekly school assemblies (for which girls had to wear middy blouses and red ties) didn't belong to this school. The "new" school seemed modern, although it was almost fifty years old. Our school was very old even when we went there—classroom walls had to be slid back to create the space for assemblies. Alice remembers the teachers as "pretty strict," although she once invited her favorite, Mrs. Holden, to lunch and was surprised that she came.

Alice's husband was in the service in World War II. While he was fighting, she was making large balls from rubber bands and tin foil for the war effort. Her mother was an air raid warden, and Alice remembers sitting in the halls of her apartment house during air raid drills, singing patriotic songs. She also recalls that in the early war years, or just before, a number of European refugee children joined us in our school.

Alice's father owned a manufacturing business with a factory in Alabama. Her mother never worked but was a strong influence on Alice's career decisions. She "drummed" into Alice the advantages of becoming a teacher: she could always get a job, and she could be home when her children were. Alice attributes her mother's advice to the experience of living through the Depression.

> . . . she always impressed upon me the idea of being able to earn a living and being financially independent. As a result, I became a teacher, made financial investments with my husband, and I have always been an equal partner in all our ventures and decisions. I have always believed that women should be independent and self-reliant.

Alice's family was close. Her parents lived most of their lives in the same neighborhood, and her maternal grandparents lived nearby. They were together every Friday night for the Jewish Sabbath and for all holidays. Alice reflects that her family has been the most important determinant of how she turned out as a person. She still recalls her mother saying that you should treat people nicely when you go up the ladder so they will do the same for you when you come back down.

In Julia Richman High School, Alice had been selected to be part of the elite Country School, and she concentrated on her studies to be able to remain there. She took both French and Spanish, and the teacher who taught both languages — as Madame Goldberg in French class and Señora Goldberg in Spanish — was sometimes confused about which class she was teaching when she saw Alice. Alice was serious about music, particularly playing the piano. She was also interested in boys. Finding these creatures could be a challenge since a girls' high school in the city was not strong on social activities.

After graduation, Alice left home to attend Syracuse University in upstate New York, planning to major in music. She discovered that she missed the city. It was also clear that her father missed *her*. She left after one year and returned to the city, transferring to New York University.

Alice decided to follow her mother's advice and prepare for teaching at this time, majoring in French and planning to teach at the secondary level. Eight years after graduation, after marriage and the birth of her two children, Alice returned to college for a master's degree in elementary education. She had decided that she wanted to teach younger children and was prepared to attend classes nights, Saturdays, and summers to achieve that goal. Alice says she was one of the first women in her crowd to go back to school and then out to work. Most of the women she knew didn't work at all. She reflects that she was driven by something within herself to do something more satisfying than merely staying home.

For almost thirty years, Alice taught elementary school in the same school district on Long Island, New York, where she lived. Life as a teacher is "lived by the clock," and Alice now enjoys being free of the routine of her working years. She is a serious bridge player, which she plays in her home community and in Florida, where she and her husband spend an ever-increasing part of the winter. It is, she says, "time to have fun."

Before we met, Alice asked me on the phone if I were still blonde. I laughed and said I was completely gray. For the record, although black-and-white photography doesn't reveal it, Alice is now a shimmering blonde.

Ursula BORN SEPTEMBER 8

INTERVIEWED AND PHOTOGRAPHED NOVEMBER 1, 2000

Ursula was an only child, born at home in a village in Saxony, Germany. Her father was a businessman — the owner of a factory that failed, then an employee of a large fruit and vegetable wholesaler. Her paternal grandparents were farmers and lived a couple of houses away. So did her uncle and his family. When Ursula was ten years old, she moved with her parents to nearby Freiberg and then spent all her school vacations with her grandparents on the farm. She helped out but was also permitted to climb trees and read if she wanted to. There wasn't much hugging, but she had a feeling of belonging there and she dearly loved her grandmother. An aunt on her mother's side of the family had seven children of her own and made Ursula feel she was in the way when Ursula biked over to visit, often greeting the girl with "What do you want now?"

Ursula started school in the village. When the war started in 1939, the male teachers were drafted and retired teachers took over. On the recommendation of one of them, Ursula went to an academic high school (*Gymnasium*) in Freiberg. She was still in school when the war ended. Ursula doesn't feel that the war interfered much with her life. Her father was in the army at first but was released as an employee in the "essential" business of food distribution. Her family never went hungry. Their relatives on the farm kept them supplied with potatoes, even butter.

Ursula is very conscious of the role politics has played in her life: "I lived through two dictatorships from beginning to end. The first one — the Hitler dictatorship — barely influenced my life. It came during my childhood."

The Russians came in 1945 and her school building became a military hospital. Ursula was transferred to a vocational school, where she was miserable because she couldn't study mathematics and science. One day she declared, "I won't go to school anymore!" and received the first spanking in her life. The next day she found a letter from her father, permitting her to leave that school. The following year, the Gymnasium reopened and she completed the course of study in 1950.

Ursula always had school friends but remembers being often disappointed by them. They would promise to come by and she would wait all day. They had brothers and sisters for company, forgetting that she was alone.

Although Ursula herself had never been to a doctor, she wanted to become a doctor and to care for children. She thinks this desire came from caring for a baby who lived in the same house, starting when Ursula was only eight. She studied medicine at the University of Jena in Thuringen for six "carefree student years."

Ursula wrote, "The second dictatorship [the East German communist regime] touched me very personally." In 1956 she went to Dresden for further specialized study. There she met and fell in love with a physician from West Germany who had also come to Dresden for study in his specialty. He was married but said he intended to divorce his wife. For the next ten years, their hopes and prospects reflected the politics of their divided country. In 1961 the Berlin Wall was built. East Germany had suffered a massive departure of physicians to the West in the years before, but the Wall put an end to that and was even a barrier to a West German returning home. Ursula's lover immediately applied for permission to leave, a process that took two years of intensive negotiations.

Ursula had seen many friends and colleagues leave for the West before the Wall but had never considered leaving: "My homeland was here, my mother, my work." But Ursula was in love and she badly wanted to have a child. She started the lengthy process to get permission to leave the country, battling the bureaucracy for four years. The lovers were able to meet in East Berlin from time to time. They were planning a vacation to Budapest in 1967 when Ursula discovered that he was seeing a new woman. The end was something of a relief, she says, but it had taken ten years of her life!

At thirty-eight, Ursula married another physician, and in 1971 her daughter was born. Ursula had been practicing medicine in Dresden before her marriage. Afterward, she moved to the village of Kohren, the "smallest city in Saxony," where her husband had a practice; they both practiced there until after unification in 1992. The years in Kohren ended bitterly when the owner of the house in which they lived and practiced, who had left for the West years ago, returned after unification to claim the property. They were evicted.

Still, it gives Ursula pleasure to relate that her daughter, a gifted musician who was studying in Leipzig in 1989, was "among those who demonstrated for democracy and the freedom to travel." She describes the unification of the country—often called the "transition" (*Wende*) in Germany—as a "great marvel . . . a great good fortune . . . And so far I have had ten years to find my way among the joys and perils of freedom and the struggles of democracy."

Nevertheless, the move from Kohren to Dresden and all the life changes that accompanied it were difficult to adjust to. At first, Ursula was depressed: "No Kohren, no work, no child." The departure from the small town had not been happy. Ursula was retired. The nest was empty since her daughter was pursuing a demanding career as a professional cellist. Then Ursula discovered painting in a class for seniors—the same class that Edith takes—and was overcome with enthusiasm for making art. It remains a source of pleasure and energizing challenge for her. In letters that we have exchanged since our meeting in Dresden, Ursula has reported on the different art media and art genres she and the class have attempted and on the exhibition of the best work of the class in 2001.

Ursula's letters also tell me about her trips and are accompanied by post-cards and photographs. She and her husband are discovering the previously closed-off world through travel, which they do as much as they can while they still can, they say. Ursula is finding her way.

Thelma BORN SEPTEMBER 26

INTERVIEWED AND PHOTOGRAPHED NOVEMBER 15, 2000

When Thelma contacted me, she began by writing, "It's been a long jig," but she has "enjoyed almost every minute." The second of seven children, Thelma was born in Monti, Iowa, an entirely Irish Catholic community at that time. Across the Buffalo River was an Irish Protestant town. Thelma's great-grandparents came from Ireland to Iowa via Kentucky. She is very proud of her Irish heritage. Ironically, she lives in a town called Norway, Iowa, and is married to a man of Norwegian descent.

Thelma's father stopped farming during the Depression and worked at a meat-packing plant and on the railroad. He had contracted polio when he was seventeen but was not very disabled by it. Her mother suffered from depression and often couldn't get out to do things. Thelma determined early in her life never to be depressed but to "take life as it comes." In high school, she was quick to laugh and liked to have a good time. She still is; she still does.

Thelma's first five years of school were in a one-room school with a single teacher. She walked over two miles to school. In winter, the children wore long, heavy, ribbed stockings, which she remembers hanging on a clothesline around the school's wood-burning stove to dry. She was left-handed but made to change. Now she is left-handed in everything except writing.

After fifth grade, the family moved to Walker and Thelma finished high school there. She particularly loved history and geography, and remembers that there were good teachers. There were only nine students in her high school graduating class. Thelma has a wartime memory of her class going out to dinner. The girls were dressed up, but since nylons weren't available, they used leg makeup. Alas, it rained and the leg makeup ran and streaked!

Thelma married at twenty-one and worked at the gas and electric company while her husband was in Korea during the war. She had a daughter, then adopted a daughter and a son. When her youngest went to kindergarten, Thelma began a twenty-five–year job as secretary to the principal in her children's school. She also ran a small travel business from home for about five years. After retiring from her school job, Thelma was elected mayor of her town three times on write-in ballots. She declined to serve the third term, but she is proud of her achievements: the city took down some old, derelict buildings on her watch, and "Christmas in Norway" was

started, with a carnival for the children. Townswomen gathered convivially, with a jug of wine, to bake cookies for the festivities.

Thelma still works, two days a month, at the billing office of the local phone company. She also volunteers in a Cedar Rapids soup kitchen and as an advocate for abused or neglected children through a court-appointed organization. She loves to travel, especially to Ireland, where she has already been three times, and is planning another trip. She is very interested in politics, her views decidedly independent of her husband's. But then, she feels she has always been independent.

Thelma supposes that women born in 1931 all learned to make do and economize, and they also learned to entertain themselves: to read, to enjoy poetry, to use their imagination. She wrote that she learned early the "pleasure of hard work."

> I have carried this with me through my life. I can think of how terrible it would be to get up in the mornings with nothing to do. I make a list every night before I go to bed of what I want to get done the next day. To spend a day doing nothing for other people — is a day wasted. The world is full of good people (and a few stinkers) so enjoy them — life is good!

Alma BORN OCTOBER 3

INTERVIEWED SEPTEMBER 6, 2001 PHOTOGRAPHED NOVEMBER 17, 2001

Although the Depression was "in full swing" when Alma was born, she says, "I always had enough to eat and to wear. I didn't realize until much later how my parents had worked and worried through those years."

Alma was an only child but had many friends in school, in church, and in the neighborhood in the Bronx, New York. She didn't go to kindergarten because her mother "couldn't bear to let [her] go," but she attended the local public school for the next eight years. It was a very large school with more than forty children to a class and several classes for each grade. It was "pretty strict" but not oppressive. After her first term, Alma was always in the -1 section (as in 4A-1, 4B-1), which was for the academically best pupils. Everyone, she says, knew what -1 meant.

In 1940, when there were more job openings for women, Alma's mother went back to work as a stenographer for General Motors. Alma's maternal grandmother lived with the family and was home for Alma when her mother was at work. Grandmother had worked in a sweatshop on the Lower East Side as a seamstress in her youth. She made all of Alma's clothes. She lived until she was ninety-eight. Alma's mother lived to be 101.

Alma recalls the "huge" public advertising effort to recruit nurses for the Cadet Nurses Corps during World War II: "As a twelve-year old, I admired the smart gray uniforms with the red trimming, and even the lipstick in Cadet Nurse Red." Although her first ambition in elementary school was to be a radio announcer, the influence of this twelve-year-old's admiration later proved decisive.

Alma was inclined toward the local coed high school but took the test for Hunter College High School and passed. At Hunter, the girls were told, "Now you are a queen among queens." Alma had a one-hour commute, by foot and by subway, and sometimes left the house for school when her mother was leaving for work. She worked on homework until 10 or 11 P.M. Because she lived so far away, she wasn't involved in activities after school, but she got all A's and graduated second in her class.

Alma perceived that "careers open to women were limited." Hunter emphasized teaching and, although several girls in her class went on to study medicine, Alma didn't feel like a "pioneer." She decided that nursing was what she wanted and assumed she would go into a hospital nursing pro-

gram. The Hunter guidance counselor was at a loss to help with such a goal, but at a church camp Alma heard about Cornell University's baccalaureate program, which was situated in the city with the university's medical school rather than in upstate New York with the other Cornell colleges.

Cornell required two years of undergraduate work before accepting students into the nursing program. Alma lived at home and went to Queens College, one of the city colleges. On the first day of classes in her first course, Alma met the man who became her husband. He was studying history and intended to become an Episcopal priest. They were married after her graduation from Cornell, just before she was twenty-three.

Alma reflects, "We both wanted a large family, and that was the norm in the fifties. I loved nursing and was able to work part-time wherever we lived until our four children were older." Indeed, she worked until she was eight months pregnant with the first child, took only one month off, and worked throughout her pregnancies with the other three. There are less than eight years between the first child and the last.

Alma says of herself that she had more energy than her four children required and that she had to use that energy. When we sat at lunch together with her husband, Alma reiterated that it would have been hard for the family if she hadn't been able to use up her energy professionally. Her husband laughed and vigorously agreed. She credits the Hunter experience; Hunter, she says, "enabled you to do a lot of things well."

At first, Alma moved and found employment in her field wherever her husband's vocation took them: to Philadelphia for seminary, then to Queens after he was ordained, then back to Philadelphia. She worked in hospitals in pediatrics and obstetrics. In 1962, looking for full-time work, she discovered that her Cornell degree qualified her to teach. This was a new idea to her and a new turning. She became an instructor and worked evenings, supervising and evaluating clinical work and helping with new procedures. Baby number four temporarily interrupted her teaching.

Realizing that she really liked to teach, Alma concluded that a master's degree would be necessary. She earned the degree at the University of Pennsylvania in 1965 in medical-surgical nursing with a functional emphasis in education. After her student teaching, she taught part-time at the university in the baccalaureate and master's programs for four years. In 1969 Alma's husband was interested in leaving Philadelphia, and they moved to Wildwood, New Jersey. Alma decided to work on a doctorate so that she could be a director or dean of nursing. "Why?" she asks, and answers that she was "always driven to excel," starting with her mother "pushing" her. Each generation in her mother's family has gone farther than the preceding one.

But first she worked, commuting from bucolic Wildwood to Atlantic City to teach at Atlantic Community College for five years, her first experience with an associate degree program. She "wanted to be boss" and in 1974 accepted a position at Stockton State College to develop a new upper-division program for nurses who already had associate degrees to earn their bachelor's degrees. Alma succeeded in getting the new program accredited. While still at Stockton, she began commuting to the University of Pennsylvania two evenings a week after work, earning her Ed.D. in 1980.

In 1981, after her youngest child graduated from high school, the family moved to Bloomington, Illinois, for Alma to be director of the School of Nursing at Illinois Wesleyan. It was the first move for *her* job. She stayed until 1986 and "learned a lot" about running a school, but she became "restless" and felt isolated in a location hard for the children to visit. She applied for and was hired as dean of the Georgetown University School of Nursing. This was the second family move that she initiated. At Illinois Wesleyan, Alma "did everything" administrative; at Georgetown, there were associate and assistant deans. She now says she cringes at how little she knew when she went there. She retired as dean in 1992 and from the faculty in 1996. She continues as a visiting professor at the University of Maryland and the Uniformed Services University of the Health Sciences in Bethesda.

Alma has a lengthy record of publications on nursing and nursing education issues, but in the past decade, she has become most interested in nursing history. In 2000 she published a major history of Georgetown's School of Nursing from 1903 to 2000, *Learning, Faith and Caring* (distributed by Tau Chapter, Sigma Theta Tau). She is currently doing oral histories of women members of the prestigious Cosmos Club in Washington (previously all-male), of which she is a member.

Three of Alma's four children became military officers in different branches of the armed services (the fourth is a professor of political science), and Alma wrote that she

> felt fortunate that they were serving their country in peacetime. Now we are engaged in another war [against terrorism] . . . and I fully appreciate what the families of those who served in the other wars must have suffered.

In our times, she reflects, there has been "tremendous change." There have been "material" changes—we "have much more"—and changes in attitudes about what women can do, from a couple of choices to "anything." She couldn't have accomplished what she has without her husband's support, and Alma grants that it was difficult for him. He has changed, too, from a more conservative outlook to telling her that "it's your turn."

Alice Miriam BORN OCTOBER 16

INTERVIEWED AND PHOTOGRAPHED NOVEMBER 16, 2001

Alice has lived in the Washington, D.C., area since 1956, but she was born in the borough of Queens, New York. She had a brother six years older and a sister two years younger. Another sister died in infancy before Alice was born. Her father was an engineer who worked for the city, designing subways. What could be more New York City-like than that! She fondly remembers being taken to work with him and being allowed to draw at a drafting table. She also remembers the frugality of the times: the linen used for blueprints was washed for other uses at home. Alice's mother was a social worker and always worked. In fact, she sometimes brought clients home to dinner. Alice's aunt lived with the family, together with her son, and took care of the household. Alice and her brother and sister called their aunt "Ma" and their mother by her first name, Sarah, perhaps because their cousin called her "Aunt Sarah."

Alice says that her mother was a "liberated woman," and so Alice grew up believing that women were "at least equal" to men. Her father never questioned this belief. Alice felt, as a result, that she "didn't have to prove anything." It tickles her that when her mother, at eighty-four years old, came to visit Alice and attend a social work conference, her mother reported that she "loved seeing old people so articulate and well groomed." Mother first learned to cook when she was eighty-eight and her sister could no longer do it. She explained that she followed Alice's advice and "just read the recipes." She died at ninety-five.

In elementary school, although Alice was "one of the smarter" ones, she was "not popular at all." In her typically direct way, she describes herself as a "stuffy fat kid." When she was about to enter a seventh-grade class taught by a teacher no one seemed to like, her brother urged her to judge for herself and not to prejudge. She looks back on this advice as an important lesson and a benefit of having an older brother. The worst of that term turned out to be the really bad fudge the teacher made as a treat for the class. Those late elementary school years were the war years, and Alice wrote every day to a cousin in the Coast Guard. She remembers that the mailman would ring the doorbell if he had a letter from a serviceman. And then there was the taste of kohlrabi, with which she first became acquainted "as a result of our school's

encouraging growing Victory gardens by selling us packets of seeds for one cent. It hasn't been a top priority friendship on my part."

The principal suggested to her mother that Alice take the test for Hunter College High School, and she passed. "What a place!" she says. The best part was making friends, some of whom she still sees. Alice was elected once as class representative to the student government organization. She also was cochair of the assembly committee, and her charge was to stand in front at assemblies and intone, "Flag of your country, salute!"

Alice reports that you "really learned" at Hunter because "they scared it into you." She was scared by some of the teachers and cried easily — "if someone looked at me cross-eyed." She was once told to leave the classroom and "not come back." Probably, she says, she had "sassed" the teacher. The librarian made her comfortable in the library with books to read, and she had to be called back, reluctantly, to class. Once she failed a history class because she "refused to memorize dates." She didn't like that teacher — she would "show her." The usual punishment was to be compelled to take German, an unpopular language at that time, but since Alice had studied both Latin and French, she merely had to repeat the history class. It wasn't too bad, she said; she met some new girls. Despite these adventures, which indicate a rebellious streak, the yearbook quoted Wordsworth next to her picture: "A violet by a mossy stone / Half hidden from the eye!"

Alice went to Queens College, one of the New York City colleges. She wanted to be a teacher but never took the required speech test. City standards for teachers were rigorous in this respect, and Alice had become conscious of her nasality and lisping in speech class. She sampled a number of majors, finally graduating with a French major. After college, Alice, her sister, and a friend went on a three-month jaunt to Europe for which they had worked and saved.

After working for about a year for *Woman's Day* magazine, she passed a city test to be a "college office assistant." Marriage intervened and then Alice joined the Office of the Dean of Students at Brooklyn College. The place was a "disaster." The student records were in piles on the floor. Alice says she "liked to put things in order" and, although she faced some "hassles," people were amazed at how she straightened up the office and filled requests for records without the delays they had grown accustomed to. Alice's husband was working for the Social Security Administration. In 1956 they moved to Washington, D.C., where they both worked for the government, he in the Census Bureau (later returning to Social Security), she in the Navy Hydrographic Office as a typist.

Between 1957 and 1963, they had four children, three boys and a girl, and Alice didn't return to paid employment for some time. She kept busy, however, as an active volunteer in ways that expressed her compassion and idealism, with the League of Women Voters and the Suburban Maryland Fair Housing Board. She became Director of Community Relations for the latter organization, working to give community support to Black families who were moving into white neighborhoods and to prepare white families for the changing neighborhood. She served on subcommittees of the county Human Relations Commission and worked as a tenant aide for the Housing Authority.

Alice says her aim was to be a housewife, perhaps because her mother wasn't. Mother never neglected the children, but she never stopped working. Bringing clients home to dinner showed both her professional involvement and the family value of gathering people together and feeding them. Alice herself did return to paid employment, and for the past twenty years she has been a part-time proofreader at a publishing firm. She doesn't intend to retire until there is something she really prefers to do. She now finds herself like her mother in being the focal point of the family and like both mother and grandmother in her intentness on gathering people together and feeding them.

Alice was widowed in 1998: "one of the worst days of my life." Several paintings by her husband are displayed in her house. Two of her four grown children live in California and two live with her. They are all single. She has been active in her synagogue over a long period, holding many offices, and is currently the coordinator of study groups. She is also devoted to the Hunter alumnae association. She is now the coordinator of the food subgroup of the local chapter. Food is obviously important to her. She wryly comments that she "has the girth to prove it." I personally benefited from her focus, being served a delicious hot lunch and, after photographing, tea and homemade sweets.

Sandra BORN OCTOBER 21

INTERVIEWED JUNE 13, 2001 PHOTOGRAPHED NOVEMBER 15, 2001

Sandra believes that "we have lived during dramatic times . . . all keenly aware of our responsibilities to the society in which we live." Her mother was active in neighborhood politics in New York, as well as in the Parent Teacher Association (PTA) at Sandra's school. She was as committed a Republican as Sandra's father was a loyal Democrat. Politics was something they discussed at home. Perhaps because of this background, Sandra has many memories of World War II.

When she heard about Pearl Harbor, Sandra was frightened and expected to be bombed. There were air raid drills, including one where the children were sent home. (I remember this one, too. I have always wondered why they sent children out on the streets — would they have done that in a *real* air raid?) Sandra's mother was not at home that day, and Sandra chose to stay with the elevator operator of her building. "I wanted to die with someone I knew," she says. Both her parents were air raid wardens. Sandra followed the news, locating events on National Geographic maps. One relative was killed, one missing, and one was a prisoner of war.

Sandra was the oldest of three children but a brother, two years younger, died at two and a half years from spinal meningitis. Her sister was seven years younger. When Sandra and her sister had whooping cough and had to stay out of school for six weeks, Sandra remembers her mother taking them both on excursions around New York.

There were two grandmothers. Her paternal grandmother was a "remarkable matriarch" who lived to be ninety-six. Although she spoke broken English, having come to the States from Poland as a young bride, she was a commanding presence. Sandra's maternal grandmother, who died when Sandra was ten, is remembered for the gifts she invariably brought: sour balls in a glass jar and underpants.

Sandra was always happy in school and skipped a term in seventh grade. She "loved learning for learning's sake" and was accepted into Hunter College High School. It "opened the whole world" for her to be with classmates who were all highly motivated.

Because her parents could not afford to send her away to college, Sandra went to Hunter College, one of the city colleges, with the understanding that she could go away to summer schools. Her first summer she went to the

University of Wisconsin with a friend. She loved her first time out of New York City and found it "romantic, exciting, beautiful." There were attractions outside of summer school classes, including her first experience with dating.

The second summer was even more fateful. Sandra was approached by the campus Jewish student organization, Hillel, to attend a camp for young adults, fully paid, in North Carolina; the camp was Hillel's effort to involve Jewish students more in Hillel activities. Sandra met a "young man from Greensboro" who asked her to go home with him to meet his family at the end of the summer. She loved Greensboro — it was "warm, lovely" — and she loved the young man as well. They dated through their remaining college years, traveling in turn to see each other. Sandra graduated one year ahead of him and applied to the University of North Carolina, where he went to school, as well as to Duke University, for a master's degree in American history. She was accepted by both schools, but her parents felt it was better for them to be on separate campuses since they weren't yet married. So Sandra spent one year at Duke and completed everything except the thesis before her wedding. She still regrets the unfinished degree.

Then, in 1953, this New York City girl took up married life in Chapel Hill, North Carolina, where her husband started law school. Sandra's mother had gone to a "normal school" to study education, and although she hadn't ever taught, she advised Sandra, "train to be a teacher!" Sandra taught English and social studies at a county high school for two years, after which she found herself pregnant. Birth control was "not so reliable" then, and this development was difficult for the young couple with the husband still in school. Their parents were able to help financially, and Sandra worked at home after her son was born, editing manuscripts and compiling and grading tests. After her husband finished his law studies, they moved back to

Greensboro, where he started practicing law. Sandra found a babysitter and worked as a bank teller until her daughter was born at the end of 1958.

For the next twenty years, Sandra and her family lived a stable and happy suburban life. Sandra did not have paid employment but was extremely active in both the religious and secular communities of Greensboro. She was president of the sisterhood of her synagogue, as well as of the PTA, and worked for the school libraries and special school programs in creative writing. She belonged to an "auxiliary" of wives of town lawyers. She worked for a peaceful transition during desegregation. She had a "fantastic" opportunity to write book reviews for the local newspaper and women's clubs. Her husband's practice flourished, and they were part of the social scene of long-established Jewish families in Greensboro.

Good things may not last forever. When Sandra was almost fifty, and her children in college or beyond, circumstances changed and led her and her husband to look elsewhere to carry on their lives. They moved to Washington, D.C., where her husband started a second career as an attorney in the U.S. Labor Department. In Greensboro, Sandra had taken a typing course and started to work for a real estate company. Now in Washington, she felt "traumatized" that she "had lost the life" she knew and where she was known. Facing the challenge to her sense of self-worth, she had to make a "second beginning."

With help from a friend she had known in high school, Sandra found work as a researcher for the book division of *U.S. News & World Report*. Then, in 1982, she began a twelve-year career in the U.S. Commerce Department, starting as an assistant to a political appointee who "really needed a Jewish mother" and eventually attaining career status, retiring in 1994 as the director of the Management Services Division. Sandra is pleased that her work there drew on all her skills and past experience.

It took ten years for Sandra and her husband to get securely on their feet after Greensboro. For the five years after her retirement, "everything was going beautifully"; they were "fabulous" years. Then her husband's cancer diagnosis in 2000 and his laryngectomy early in 2001 devastated her. He continues to work with great determination, but Sandra suffers with the stress of his condition.

Sandra : 125

She keeps busy as an active volunteer at the library, synagogue, and an art museum. She plays tennis, bridge, and mah jongg (with her mother's tiles). Sandra says that the loss of security she suffered earlier has made her a stronger and more adaptable person, yet she says that she fears growing old, fears losing the ability to do all the things she wants to.

In the spirit of making the most of the present, Sandra and her husband decided to act on their dream of taking a long vacation in southern France. They spent two months in a town near Nice in the spring of 2002, and Sandra reported that it was a glorious, memorable time. They both felt "totally rejuvenated" and plan to go again.

Jackie BORN OCTOBER 27

INTERVIEWED JUNE 5 AND 8, 2001 PHOTOGRAPHED SEPTEMBER 14, 2001

I met Jackie in her chambers as a Supreme Court justice for Nassau and Suffolk counties, New York. Not intending to retire until the last permissible year, when she is 76, Jackie "loves the law—how it helps me to think," and she finds being a judge "magical."

But her story begins differently: "I remember my parents' struggle to retain their dignity—and feed and clothe two children. My father held two jobs all the time." Those jobs included selling Good Humor ice cream bars and helping out at catered events in a New York hotel. He was able to bring home ice cream and leftover food as "treats" for the family. After World War II began, he did better with a job at the Brooklyn Navy Yard. Jackie remembers wearing cast-off clothes and not being "properly" dressed for class trips in elementary school. But elementary school in the Bronx was not a happy experience for other reasons as well. She talked too much in class and was compared unfavorably with her three-year-older brother, who was an "angel." (At home, there was the memory of another "angel," the sister who died in infancy six years before Jackie was born.) In singing class, she was humiliatingly declared a "listener."

When Jackie was eight years old, her mother went back to work as a secretary, commuting by subway. Jackie and her brother became latchkey kids. Their father, who worked nights then, was sleeping when they came from school, and they were responsible for shopping and cooking dinner to be ready when Mother came home.

After junior high, Jackie took and passed the test to enter Hunter College High School, where she encountered the "first defining experience of life." Everything about it opened up her world. Getting out of the largely Jewish Bronx neighborhood and going to school by subway was an eye opener. There were girls from all over the city, girls who were Black, Asian, non-Jewish. It was not a perfect world: she recalls hearing twenty years later that a Black classmate didn't get to a committee meeting held in someone's apartment house because she was directed to the service entrance when she showed up, and went home instead.

Jackie was active at Hunter on the newspaper staff, in plays and, above all, in athletic activities as president of the Athletic Association. She was (and is)

very tall and, for the first time, she felt "free to be physical." She concedes that she probably didn't take full advantage of Hunter's academic opportunities.

There was no money for going to a private college, and Jackie went on to Hunter College, a city college, after high school. At the beginning of her second year, her mother, forty-six years old, had a stroke; Jackie stayed home for six months to take care of her. "Oh my, what a tough lady," Jackie says of her mother. With a "barrage" of letters to city agencies, her mother demanded and received rehabilitation and then a city job. She had the use of only one arm and had to commute to work with a brace on her leg and a tripod cane.

After that interruption in her education, Jackie attended classes at the Bronx campus of Hunter in the morning, worked as a secretary in the afternoon, and had classes at Hunter's Manhattan campus from 6 to 10 P.M. She got all A's. After that year, she balanced a full-time job during the day with night classes for four hours, four nights a week.

In the summer of 1951, Jackie met the man who became her husband, and she left college to get married about a year before graduating. She didn't return to school until sixteen years and four children later. She wrote about the fatefulness of meeting him: he "shap[ed] my adult life in ways I couldn't have imagined. He helped me grow—and he recognized me as a woman, as a person of value."

When her youngest started school, Jackie returned to college on Long Island, where she lived. This was 1968, and C. W. Post College was trying to interest adults in returning to school. Most of Jackie's previous course work was credited, and when she graduated three years later, her family proudly attended commencement. Earlier, Jackie's mother had told her that her career choices were to be a nurse, teacher, or librarian (interestingly not mentioning her own secretarial work). Jackie chose librarian and earned a master's degree in library science in 1973. She immediately discovered that a librarian was not what she wanted to be, after all, and instead worked for the Council on Foreign Relations and as a public relations volunteer for the local high school theater group.

"Floundering" in the mid-1970s, she took seriously a suggestion made at a party that she go to law school. Her husband encouraged her, and her children tutored her in math for the entrance exam. During her legal education at St. John's University, Jackie's house was the center of a study group of three or four fellow students, young men who usually stayed for dinner, chatting with the children while she took time off to do laundry. Their presence in the house energized Jackie's husband, who had a "wonderful mind" but had never gone to college, to write a book on rare coins—the family business in which he was engaged.

After Jackie earned her law degree in 1979, she got the job she wanted, Assistant District Attorney for Nassau County. She appreciated the diversity in her office, where every background, age, and handicap were represented. After seven years, she went into private practice as a criminal defense lawyer, then as an appellate attorney. In 1991, when her husband was suffering from prostate cancer, Jackie took a job as administrator of an assigned counsel defender plan. Since her office was five minutes from her home, it freed her to be available to him as needed. He died near the end of 1992.

Jackie continued in that job through 1996 and began running for office, seeking to become a judge. Defeated four times, she succeeded in being elected a district court judge in November 1996. She served only four years of a six-year term because she was then elected to the New York State Supreme Court, where she now serves. Her court deals with matrimonial cases and, although she recognizes a "basic sadness" to the substance of the work, she is proud of her court and of her "top notch" all-female staff.

Jackie is tall and slim and moves athletically. She is struck by the difference in "physical activity level" between our generation and our mothers'.

> I never knew my parents or in-laws to engage in any kind of physical activity . . . (unless you include shopping). Today we do just about everything young people do, only maybe slower.

Jackie and her three daughters, now forty-four, forty-two, and thirty-nine, took a hiking vacation together in Yellowstone National Park in the summer of 2001, testimony to this difference.

Since the 1970s, Jackie has had a "sense of change in the status of women," and she imagines that other women her age recognize this change as well. "Who I am today is not who I was," she says. Yet the woman she is today is also the proud grandmother of fifteen grandchildren, whose photographs are prominent in her chambers.

Jacci BORN NOVEMBER 1

INTERVIEWED AND PHOTOGRAPHED JANUARY 6, 2002

Jacci is a New Yorker who moved to Sarasota, Florida, in 1994. She teases me in e-mails about Thanksgiving dinner and winter social events "around the pool" in eighty-degree temperatures, often adding a conciliatory "(smile)". She has an active social life, which includes a large number of New York friends who also retired to Sarasota. She loves "her" lake on the beautiful grounds outside her door (except for the occasional interloping alligator). Yet she reflects that as a young African American woman, she would never have imagined choosing to live in the South: "Who would have believed in 1931 that I would be living as a retiree in an integrated middle-class neighborhood and church in Sarasota, Florida??"

Jacci was born in her grandmother's house in Rockville Center, Long Island, just as her mother had been. From that start, her grandmother continued to be very important in Jacci's life. She was called Nana and was the matriarch of the family.

> She set the tone for behavior and values. Nana insisted on us doing well in school and in other endeavors. [She] taught me to read when I was four years old so I started Kindergarten reading ahead of everyone else. She was an in-charge person and was well known in town . . . I find myself quoting Nana even today . . . She had a profound influence on my life and I think I am very much like her.

Jacci remembers her grandmother sitting in a rocking chair crying "as if the rug had been pulled from under her" when President Roosevelt died in 1945. A New Deal program had saved her house from foreclosure.

Jacci was always a good student, a "well-balanced" child. The elementary school she attended, however, was a "segregated school in the north." School district lines had been drawn so that the school population was completely Black. The white children who lived in that neighborhood were from Italian families and went to Catholic schools. When she was about eight, it came out that the children in Jacci's school were being taught "domestic skills"—how to set tables for the girls, shop for the boys—because they "might not get through high school." Some of the parents went to the next town's chapter of the National Association for the Advancement of Colored People, since the organization had no chapter in Rockville Center. A two-day protest strike was organized. In 1940 the parents' group prevailed in court and a new integrated school was built. By then, Jacci was in an integrated high school.

In high school, Jacci was "smart, friendly, outgoing." An "avid reader" who had started going to the library when she was seven, Jacci did well in school. She took Latin and was inducted into the National Honor Society. She was also in a service club whose members helped out in the school office and in a girls' competitive performance group. She had many friends in school, but they were "school-only" friends.

Jacci knew she wanted to be a nurse after her hospital experience for a tonsillectomy at age seven. Service had always been important to her, as expressed in her school years by membership in Girl Scouts and 4-H. When the time came to make applications in her senior year, Jacci applied only to the nursing program at Bellevue Hospital in New York City on the strength of her family doctor's advice. This doctor, who came to Rockville Center when Jacci was six or seven, "was a role model for our little community." "Trusted and caring," the doctor was often sought out for his advice. Jacci was rejected by Bellevue and "crushed" that graduation was approaching and she had no place to go. Bellevue had evaluated her required physical exam and claimed that it showed a heart murmur and that the "strain" of nursing would be too much for her. Jacci's doctor gently explained the quota system to her and its likely role in her rejection. She then applied to Massachusetts General and Philadelphia General and was accepted by both. She chose Philadelphia because the family had a good friend who lived in the city, and Jacci's mother thought it best to go where you knew someone.

Jacci loved nursing training despite the strict rules, curfews, and the hateful black stockings and black oxfords the student nurses were required to wear. In the physical exam after her first year, a particular "electrical" heart syndrome showed up. She was advised not to smoke or drink too much coffee and that was that. She worked in Philadelphia one year after her studies, then took and passed her licensure exam with a specialty in medical nursing.

Returning to Rockville Center, Jacci worked at a hospital in Queens and became an assistant head nurse in a little more than a year. She was working mainly on the 3 to 11 P.M. shift plus weekends, which prevented her from having a social life. She was also discomfited by the chronic understaffing,

which affected treatment of patients. In her studies, she had liked public health so she accepted a job with standard office hours at the Nassau County Department of Health, taking night courses in public health at Columbia University Teachers College. She carried on in this way for seven years. At least she had her weekends free.

In 1963 a friend who was a school nurse told Jacci about an opening for a school nurse in Great Neck, an affluent Long Island town. The school was eager to interview her, but Jacci put them off while she and two girlfriends went on a planned two-week vacation down South "to see what it was like before everything changed." It was a year in which one could see that things were changing. In fact, Jacci and her friends didn't observe the expected signs of segregation in the places they visited. On her return, she interviewed for the Great Neck job, which was promptly offered to her. The county health department agreed to give her a leave of absence so she could come back if she chose after one year. She took the school nursing job and only left when she retired in 1988.

The children were "bright and alert," and many parents and teachers there had

a commitment to Social Justice [and] were willing to be proactive in their beliefs . . . There was a very clear commitment to recognize the role of the Public School to be relevant to the social needs of children and we had many causes that we supported after school.

Jacci also had the freedom to think for herself and to implement her ideas. She taught sex education and started a bike safety program. When Great Neck had an influx of poorer families to a welfare hotel, Jacci was involved with the children there in an afterschool studies program. Great Neck was "an interesting place to be."

The year Jacci became a school nurse, 1963, was also the year of the March on Washington and Martin Luther King, Jr.'s famous "I Have a Dream" speech. Jacci "desperately" wanted to go to the march. She had been active in the Long Island Committee for Defense of Martin Luther King and Struggle for Freedom in the South, a religiously and racially mixed group. They raised money "all over Long Island" for civil rights causes. She asked her Baptist minister to organize a bus for the trip to Washington, but he was a conservative man who thought King "should take care of his own parish," so Jacci went along with the bus chartered by a Presbyterian church. She changed churches after that, too. Being in Washington was all Jacci had expected—an "epiphany" for her to be part of that "great feeling of love." King's assassination in 1968 was "like a stab in the heart." Jacci says that when she was a young woman, she couldn't have imagined the "changes in job opportunities for me as an African American and a Woman." At seventy, however, she finds herself "a little disappointed."

> I was naïve enough to believe that we would have solved the "race issue" by now . . . However, the racial profiling, problems with police, the lagging behind of so many still in poverty . . . are all indications that there is much to be done.

Jacci continued working in Great Neck but moved to New York to live. She met the man who became her husband in the elevator of the new co-op in Harlem to which she had recently moved. They married in 1972 when she was forty. Jacci had had a hysterectomy a few years earlier. She and her husband adopted a son. These times were perhaps the happiest of her life.

Church was always important in Jacci's life. In the early 1990s, she served as moderator of the Metropolitan Association of the United Church of Christ. She traveled all over the boroughs of New York and beyond to participate in ordinations and installations, and remarks, "What a great time I had." In Sarasota, she is very active in the Congregational Church and was just elected moderator. She recently received an award as "Honored Laywoman" from the national church synod of the United Church of Christ. She is proud that

Our denomination was founded by the Pilgrims. Women were eligible for ordination since the mid-1800s. They were on the forefront of the Abolitionist movement and established many Black colleges throughout the South . . .

Women of our age, Jacci thinks, like things done a "certain way" but are "not exactly opinionated" and don't resent those who don't think as they do. She believes in dressing up to go to church, being quiet in the theater, and having manners, but she doesn't always observe that behavior around her. Talking about old times is good but

. . . we don't want to give up yet — we are interested in learning things, in politics, and we want to make a difference.

Each of us in our own relationships has to touch the humanity in others in a way that goes beyond race, ethnicity, nationality, and religion. Otherwise we are doomed to destruction. I refer to 9/11/01.

Pat BORN NOVEMBER 19

INTERVIEWED AND PHOTOGRAPHED OCTOBER 19, 2001

Pat has lived in the town of Swansea in Wales her entire life. An only child, she was very close to her parents. Her father was a medic during World War II, serving in the North African campaign. He was mostly quiet about his wartime experiences, but Pat knows that he was once on a torpedoed ship and had to swim to safety past floating corpses. Pat's mother had worked as a shorthand-typist before she was married, and then returned to work during the war, making Pat a latchkey child. What comes first to Pat's mind, thinking of the war years, is that she felt "lonely."

Pat lived through the wartime bombings with everyone else in Swansea. She remembers that she sometimes stayed at her grandparents' and slept in a prefabricated metal bomb shelter half-buried in the back yard. Swansea suffered forty-three bombing raids between June 1940 and February 1943. The most memorable were the raids on three successive nights in February 1941. The first "flattened the town," the second hit near the steelworks not far from where Pat's grandparents lived, and the third destroyed one whole area (Mayhill) as the planes aimed for the docks. Pat was not in a shelter that third night but was hiding under the stairs with her mother and a friend who had come to play. Their house lost all its windows and doors when a bomb exploded on the street, two houses away.

When Pat's father was demobilized, he first worked for the highway department, then "worked in the evenings to better himself" while he sold goods door-to-door from a motorcycle. After that, he and Pat's mother opened a shop, a general store, in a municipal housing development.

Pat had passed the "eleven-plus" exam, used by Great Britain at the time to separate children at eleven years old into different streams of secondary education. She went to what was called "grammar school," the more academic stream, and came to feel "I'm as good as anyone else," encouraged in this feeling by her parents. She favors the old system over the contemporary "comprehensive" schools, which don't separate children at so young an age. "Not everyone is the same," she believes, and "it is better to compete . . . to try to achieve more."

After her school years, Pat worked at an office job for the city council until she married in 1954. Her mother had urged her to learn shorthand and typing, but Pat didn't care to. She bore two sons, one in 1957 and one

in 1960. Because there were many things she wanted to improve around her house, Pat took a part-time job when her younger son was about two. For eight years she worked three evenings a week as a barmaid. This schedule made it possible for her husband, a draftsman, to be home with the boys. She remarked that men don't respect women today as they did in those days. Even as a barmaid, she felt respected. The men would apologize to her if they used "the kind of language men do."

Around 1970, Pat's parents said to her, "The children don't need you [at home during the day]. Come work in the shop." And so she did, for more than five years. During that time, her husband left and they were divorced in 1974. In 1975 her mother died from breast cancer. Her father "missed her [mother] so much" that Pat took to stopping by every evening "to tuck him in." She was happy for him when he remarried, to a close friend of her mother's. Soon after, he closed the shop and Pat took a job as a receptionist at a central clinic of the Health Authority, where she worked until she retired in 1991.

Pat had a "gentleman friend" whom she met shortly after her divorce. He wanted to marry her but she chose not to. Her boys were still at home and, besides, she said, you "lose trust." They were together as good friends until he died in 1992. She took leave from her job to care for him in his final illness. With a touch of irony, she noted that her ex-husband, who had a "roving eye," was on his third marriage.

Pat's sons and their families also live in Swansea, and she is busy as a grandmother. I met her at her granddaughters' school on the day before our appointment; she is often the one to pick them up.

Pat is the sort of person whose smile is her natural expression. She has a rosy English complexion. Despite her bad knees, which have to cope with the extremely steep steps outside her house and the steep stairs inside, she avers that "I feel I've lived at the best time." Her contentment with her age and the world as it was when she was young is balanced by her dismay at the "vulgarity" of television. She calls herself the "chauffeuse" for a group of women friends, saying she doesn't go for words that blur gender differences. Pat wrote,

> Being born when people had very little, I appreciate the simpler things in life, walking in the park and at the seaside, a small bird taking food from my hand, laughter of my grandchildren. My pets too have meant a lot to me. I have been rich with family and friends.

Althea BORN NOVEMBER 25

INTERVIEWED AND PHOTOGRAPHED JANUARY 17, 2002

Althea was born in Brooklyn, an only child. Her mother's mother, who lived with the family, came to the United States from Barbados. Her father's family was from Trinidad. Althea's father worked in the business office of Anaconda Copper in Manhattan until he retired in 1985. He was "so distinguished," a gregarious man who knew many famous athletes, musicians, and other performers. Active in competitive bowling, he was instrumental in overturning the all-white membership rule of the American Bowling Congress (ABC) in 1961 and was elected to the ABC Hall of Fame in 1994. Althea's mother was a dressmaker who worked in the Manhattan garment district and also sewed at home. Observing her parents, "especially my mother," work so hard instilled the "work ethic" in Althea and, on the other hand, the determination to enjoy life when she grew older.

Althea's grandmother worked as a domestic for a Jewish family in Brooklyn, after a while living-in with them. Althea remembers staying at their house sometimes and playing with the daughter who was close to her in age. Nanny (as her grandmother was called by everyone) was invited to play a part in the son's bar mitzvah. Nanny and the family stayed in touch with each other for years, even after Nanny's employer, widowed and then remarried, moved to Florida.

Althea went to elementary school in a racially mixed neighborhood as one of the minority. She made a best friend in first grade with whom she is still close, skipped third grade, and organized friends after school to write and put on plays. She was a latchkey kid, going home alone to lunch. Junior high was a trolley trip away. Althea started getting "intimidated" there, thinking "everyone was so smart!"

She has memories from the years of World War II. Althea's father was in the Navy, stationed at an ammunition depot in Lincoln, Nebraska. The family heard on the radio about an explosion at his base. Father called to reassure them, saying only that he had been "blown out of [his] chair."

Nylons were almost mythical during the war. Althea wanted rayon stockings, but her mother bought her thick cotton lisle ones instead and a garter belt to hold them up. Thinking she was "hot stuff" anyway, she "strutted" into class and, as she walked past a boy, a garter fell to the floor—to his amusement and her extreme embarrassment. We were at that age when such

things mattered, but we were also capable of deeper feelings. She remembers crying with her girlfriends when President Roosevelt died in 1945. He was the only president they had known. She also remembers a "feast" she helped prepare with another family to celebrate V-J Day, to be ready when the two mothers came home from work.

Althea began to take piano lessons when she was five or six. A teen neighbor had taken her along to her piano lessons, and Althea was captivated. When she was fourteen, she met the singer Ruby Green at church and learned a gospel piano-playing style from her. Ruby Green remained a mentor to Althea; a large reproduction of a wonderful painting of her by James Chapin hangs on the stair landing in Althea's house. At the end of eighth grade and again at the end of ninth, Althea auditioned for admission to Music and Art High School, a selective specialized public school. She was not accepted, most likely because of a quota system. At Franklin K. Lane High School, on the border between Brooklyn and Queens, they knew all about her musical talent from the records of her Music and Art auditions. In high school, she played the clarinet and violin and was in the orchestra. In her senior year, she was the piano soloist in a performance of Gershwin's *Rhapsody in Blue*. Although she had thought of becoming a social worker, her goal became teaching music. The possibility of a concert career was also in her mind.

Althea was only sixteen when she graduated from high school. Before going on, she waited one year, during which she studied chemistry at a private school. In high school, she had been friendly, outgoing, and studious, but a loner, not a "joiner." She was always a "very obedient child." Her parents had "instilled" in her that if you were Black and had darker skin, you had to be ten times better than anyone else. It was something like a caste system in the Black community. Althea says she didn't have that much confidence anyway: she wasn't the "best" student.

Accepted by New York University in Music Education, Althea describes her time there as an "awakening." To her dismay, she learned that the piano was not considered a "major instrument," but she also discovered that she "had a voice." She studied voice as a soprano, learning in a later audition that she was really a contralto. At a high-powered soirée, a famous voice teacher told her that she might be the second "voice in a lifetime," after the renowned Marian Anderson. Althea says, without regret, that she was "not up to it," although perhaps if she had stayed single . . .

Word went around that the New York City schools were dropping music as a subject. Althea responded by taking more education courses. She didn't do student teaching because a professor told her she "wasn't teaching material." Undeterred, she taught as a substitute for five years, eventually with a permanent "sub" license. She was teaching fourth grade, a "very bright" class, in a school using a new reading program with outside reading. She "enjoyed it so!"

Althea had married not long after graduation. Her husband was a Korean War veteran and was in college. She was asked to accompany her fourth-grade class to fifth grade but she became pregnant and started to miscarry, so she had to stop teaching. The pregnancy came to term and a daughter was born in 1960. A son followed a year later. Althea stayed at home with the children when they were small.

The family had moved to Hempstead in Nassau County, which was known for having music programs in all the schools. Althea started substitute teaching. Then the principal at her school told her to gather the documentation of her teaching experience and, in the late 1960s, she transcended substitute status and was licensed to teach music and classroom subjects in grades K–12.

Starting with a part-time opening, Althea became a full-time music teacher in two schools and taught for fifteen years. When she decided to retire in 1987, somewhat disgruntled at losing her own classroom and facing the prospect of becoming "itinerant" again—pushing the piano and cart with music and books from room to room—she heard from her pupils, "we never had a music teacher like you." Althea strongly believes in what music can do, bringing out qualities in people they are unaware of. Throughout

Althea : 145

her teaching career and after retirement, Althea taught piano privately to as many as fifteen pupils at a time. She has recently reduced the number of piano pupils to her two grandsons.

Following her retirement, Althea spent nine years caregiving within the family. Her parents had divorced and her father remarried when Althea was in her twenties. Newly retired, Althea found time to be attentive to her hospitalized stepmother, then to care for her father and mother during their illnesses. She was also the daytime caregiver for her older grandson before he went to school. Her stepmother died in 1989, her father in 1998. Althea's mother moved close to her in Hempstead. Since 1995, her mother has been in a nearby nursing home, wheelchair-bound but still her "feisty" self. Her ninetieth birthday was celebrated recently with a big party at church. Althea remarked that an advantage of being an only child was being able to make the decisions about her parents as needed. As another only child, I agreed.

Althea's husband had been on the local school board from the 1970s, and Althea had been active in the Parent Teacher Association. After retirement, she says that she prayed for guidance to do something "meaningful." Soon after, she became engaged in an organized effort to defend a teacher who had been dismissed for assigning an essay to a racially mixed class on their reactions to disparaging remarks made about Black athletes by a well-known sports commentator. The group she became part of raised money, found lawyers willing to work pro bono, and went to the school hearings. The teacher was reinstated.

Althea is involved in public service projects through a sorority she joined on Long Island, and she is very active in her church at both the local and national synod level. She has moved beyond the feeling of being intimidated by others, as she was in her youth. She credits her parents for "pushing" her, her husband for having "brought her out," and a minister in the 1980s who encouraged her to take leadership roles in volunteer groups despite her initial reluctance.

Althea reflects that she is "still stuck" in racial attitudes, presuming how others view her. Is this why, when I described myself prior to our meeting at the Long Island Railroad station as gray-haired, wearing a black coat, and pulling a suitcase, she described herself as having "gray hair and brown skin"? She told me, with regret but without further explanation, that after all the years of efforts for civil rights—organized and private—she thinks the movement is "at a standstill" now.

Althea feels as if she were only in her forties or fifties and says she is "fortunate to be healthy." She and her friends are busier than some other women their age, and she likes it that way.

Roz BORN DECEMBER 8

INTERVIEWED JULY 30, 2001 PHOTOGRAPHED DECEMBER 27, 2001

I had interviewed Roz on the phone and was due to photograph her in her brokerage office near Wall Street on September 12, 2001. On September 11, she had a dramatic escape from the office, descending twenty-nine flights of stairs and ultimately walking across the Brooklyn Bridge to her home in Brooklyn Heights, covered in ash, as she told me quite calmly. Her office was relocated to temporary quarters for some weeks, and she wrote, "it is difficult without all our supporting services . . . We're managing." We ultimately got together at her Florida condo, where she and her husband spend several winter months. They take art classes there, and Roz also manages to continue working, electronically.

Yet Roz's experience in the September 11 attacks is an incidental part of her story. More unusual is that she is still working—now four days a week—as the vice president of a Wall Street firm, at the top of a ladder she started climbing as soon as she graduated from Cornell University in 1953.

> I was always told that I could do anything that I wanted to do, so I was pretty sure that I could get an interesting job if I tried hard enough.
> I knew I did not want to be a nurse or a teacher. I briefly considered going to business or law school but I was very anxious to get out to the real world of New York. I expected to support myself . . .

Roz was born in Schenectady in upstate New York, where her father, a toolmaker, worked for General Electric. During the Depression, his hours were cut to one week in six, and in 1936 he and his wife opened a retail appliance store. Roz's mother had worked in a dress shop before joining her husband in the business and was a model for Roz of a wife and mother not staying at home. There is also a connection, as she sees it, with her Jewish family background: "Jews have a long history of wives helping in the store or running the store while their husbands studied." In Poland her maternal grandmother did just that, even working on her own after her grandfather, a scholar, emigrated to this country and before the family was reunited here.

Roz's childhood was marked by her parents' necessary frugality in hard times. They were poor, but so was everyone they knew. Roz "treasured" her two dolls and her ten-cent pony ride every Sunday when the family dressed up to walk in the park. The frugality rubbed off on her: "I learned that it was

important to be practical and to become financially independent. I did not want to be subject to circumstances beyond my control."

Roz feels she was cut out for a career in sales by her early engagement with her parents' business. Before the appliance store, her father repaired used refrigerators at home and her mother sold them from the back porch. One evening when her parents were out, people came to look at a refrigerator. The babysitter knew nothing about it, but Roz, four years old, had watched her mother demonstrating the appliances and hopped out of bed to show the potential customers all the features. She made a sale, consummated the next day. Later, in elementary school, when the children were told that the proceeds from their paper drives would be used to purchase a large radio console, Roz went to the principal and told him her mother sold such radios in her store. Again, she made a sale.

Roz was "the brightest kid in school," and the teachers were all "wonderful" to her. She went to the less good of the two Schenectady high schools, located in a poorer neighborhood, but she was a winner in the Westinghouse Science Talent Search. She was voted the girl "most likely to succeed" and, she says, she did. She went to Cornell University and loved its "sophistication," majoring in economics—a "logical choice" because of the family store—but also studying philosophy, history, and studio art. She was one of only two girls in her sorority who did not marry at graduation.

When Roz consulted the guidance counselor before graduation, she found separate listings of jobs for men and women. She identified her first job herself and was hired by Jack Dreyfus, founder of the Dreyfus Fund, in the research department. After six months, she became assistant to one of the partners. The firm was small, and the partners were fairly young and accustomed to taking risks. They were also Jewish, as were most of their clients, and "they saw nothing wrong with being helped by a perky young woman." After Dreyfus, Roz changed Wall Street firms several times. She says, "Once I had a book of clients, I could have gone almost anywhere." She reflects that her career has continually kept her "in touch with what's going on in the world."

Roz met her future husband at the New School, where she was taking a painting class. They married when she was twenty-four and soon had their first son, followed three years later by another. Roz took two months off before returning to work after each pregnancy, something "almost unheard of." Her bosses were cooperative but made no special arrangements. If someone was willing to work, that was fine with them. Roz found a woman to take care of the children, someone who found her own substitutes when necessary and who worked for the family for almost fifteen years. Roz and some other mothers founded a community nursery school in Brooklyn. Parents were required to contribute one day a term to helping out, and Roz managed to do that on days when the Stock Exchange was closed.

Roz has been an active volunteer on behalf of Cornell, the chair of her forty-fifth class reunion, a member of the Cornell Council, and an interviewer of aspiring students. Both of her sons graduated from Cornell. The older is now a rabbi, the younger — after working in real estate and as a sports writer — has joined her in the firm.

Roz grants that "obviously, all benefited" from the women's movement, but her own trajectory began before the movement was a gleam in an eye. She says about herself and women like her, "We did it on our own."

Tricia BORN DECEMBER 10

INTERVIEWED AND PHOTOGRAPHED OCTOBER 17, 2001

I heard about Tricia from her older daughter, who contacted me with an enticing outline of her mother's life. When I ventured three hours west of London to the village of Dawlish, Devon, where Tricia lives, I found that she did not particularly care to talk about herself. Nor did she think that being born in 1931 had influenced her life. It was her daughters and her admiration for them that mattered: "The only significant thing that did change my life was having my children."

Tricia was born at home, the last of four children, in north London. She says she was a "mistake," and her mother made her feel like one. As a mother, she took more of an interest in her two daughters than her mother took in her. She is quick to add that her older daughter, the only one who has children, is even better—"I didn't do all with my children that she does with hers."

When Tricia was five, the family moved closer to London. She attended the same school there until she was fourteen, with an interruption of more than a year when she was evacuated to Yorkshire in 1940 to escape the bombing. Her most vivid memory of Yorkshire is of helping to pick potatoes in the fields. Fourteen was the legal age to leave school at the time, and Tricia left gladly. She says she hated school. The teachers were stricter than now, and she felt the "lessons did nothing for me." She preferred sports.

As a child, Tricia had always been on the street on roller skates, and she started skating competitively at Alexandra Palace in London. It was a "huge place" with dance and exhibition halls under a big dome. Her event was speed skating in five-mile races, but she also danced on skates. This competing continued until she was about twenty.

Tricia met her first husband at Alexandra Palace and married when she was twenty-one. She had completed a three-year apprenticeship in machine embroidery and operated a sewing machine in a factory. He was a driver. They divorced when she was thirty. Two years later she remarried. She was then working in another factory, as a cutter, where her second husband was an upholsterer. Two daughters were born, and Tricia stayed home with them until the younger was seven. She delivered Meals on Wheels for two years, a job that permitted her to be home when the girls came home from school.

For seventeen years after that, she drove a van for the local government to bring the elderly and disabled to appointments and activities.

When her daughters were out on their own, Tricia left her husband for another man and moved to the west of England, to Devon, with the intention of running a retirement home. She was familiar with the beautiful seaside villages from family holidays. The retirement home idea didn't work out, but she delivered fruit and vegetables by van for a few years, stopping at sixty when the work became too heavy.

Tricia then ran a bed-and-breakfast for nine years. The house had three large double suites and two reception rooms. Guests could come and go as they pleased, but she once had to ask a woman to leave who "took over" as if it were her own house. "Lady Jane," Tricia called her. She decided to sell the b&b to rid herself of the burden of a mortgage. At the same time, she left her companion of twenty years and moved to a different Devon village, Dawlish, where she had a good friend and where her sister and surviving brother lived. Tricia says of herself that, even as a child, "I wanted to do what I wanted to do."

I spent more time with Tricia than was usual on my visits because she lived three hours by train from where I had been and three hours by train from where I was going. She fed me many meals and kindly put me up overnight in the neat house she shares with three cocker spaniel sisters ("the girls") and an independent cat. The cocker spaniels are a lively bunch and keep Tricia close to home at the same time that they provide her with entertainment and companionship.

Mary BORN DECEMBER 18

INTERVIEWED AND PHOTOGRAPHED AUGUST 28, 2000

In retirement, Mary has become interested in genealogy. As we talked about the family, she consulted a thick notebook she has compiled, so she could be sure of her facts. Mary's family consisted of two sets of twins and five younger children. Her twin brother, fifteen minutes her senior, was a "real asset" in her life: "He always made me feel that he was my keeper," and she found that a comfort. Both sets of twins were born at home in Guthrie Center, Iowa, where her father worked for a farmer.

Mary's father was in the service in World War II in the South Pacific. She remembers him writing special cards to each of the children. After the war, he drove a gas tank truck to service local gas users. Mary believes that she has inherited her outspokenness and "bully streak" from him. Mary's mother cooked for farmhands but didn't work outside the home. More than ninety years old, she is still living on her own, with a prosthetic leg after a gangrene-related amputation when she was seventy-five.

Mary and her siblings walked to a one-room school unless the weather was "really bad." If it was, their father drove them and the teacher, who lived across the road, to school with the team of horses and the wagon. When Mary was about ten, the family moved to Audubon. What she remembers most vividly is the distinctive fire escape in the high school building. It was a kind of cylinder through which you had to drop to the ground from the third floor. Certainly memorable!

Mary has some amusing recollections of school: the time a boy put his desk out the window into a tree and the principal had to retrieve it, as well as the time a boy spit onto the principal's head from a window. She doesn't recall any punishments for these infractions. She also remembers a teacher from New York who had a doctorate and taught government, sociology, and higher math. This teacher had an unusual testing method: students selected a slip from a basket, each one getting a different question to answer.

Mary was elected Christmas Queen in her senior year and, together with the mayor, distributed Christmas trees to needy families and gifts to the first baby of the new year. During high school, she worked in a restaurant, earning fifty cents for eight hours of work. At first, she washed dishes, standing on a box to reach the sink. Becoming taller as well as older, she then became a waitress. She graduated from high school at seventeen.

Mary wanted to become a nurse, but there was no money for that and, she remarked, "you couldn't take out loans for education as you now can." She is proud that her eldest granddaughter, with whom she is very close, is a nursing student. Her two older brothers didn't finish high school, and none of the other children in the family went beyond high school.

Mary and her husband grew up together, and their families all knew one another. They married when she was nineteen and he twenty-two. They had three children in the first three years, and when the youngest went to kindergarten, Mary went back to work. She did office work in the school system and in a small parts factory in Tipton, Iowa, where they still live, and then in a psychologist's office in Iowa City. She retired twice from that job, the last time in 1998.

Mary says that dealing with declining health, hers and her husband's, is a burden she didn't expect. And she can never forget the tragedy of her older son's death at age twenty-seven in a motorcycle accident. Happily, her other two children live close by.

Mary has always done volunteer work at church, and she now helps individuals with the complexities of their medical insurance claims. She enjoys e-mail correspondence with her granddaughter and with several nieces and nephews. She also likes to do jigsaw puzzles, "but not 3-D ones!" A large Beanie Babies collection is on display in the living room, where we sat to talk.

Edith BORN DECEMBER 19

INTERVIEWED AND PHOTOGRAPHED OCTOBER 30, 2000

Edith, who has lived all her life in or near Dresden, Germany, summed up her attitude toward life: "I am an optimist. I enjoy life and would still like to spend a long time on this earth."

She is thankful that her two children and two older grandchildren are all working—something not to be taken for granted these days in the former East Germany. Since they are independent, Edith can enjoy her free time in retirement, time she has passionately devoted to painting in an art class for seniors. As a young woman, she looked on women of her present age as "ancient," something that seems amusing to her now.

Edith was born at home, the second in a family of five children. Her father worked in a factory. Her mother was at home but occasionally did house-work for others. Edith was close to her maternal grandmother, who lived in a village about twenty miles from Dresden and ran a general store. Edith spent summers in the village from an early age. Before the firebombing of Dresden by Allied planes in 1945, she and her family were evacuated to Grand-mother's village and escaped the worst of the destruction in the city. Edith stayed two more years after the war, completing school there. Always good-natured and lively, she became more ambitious, leaving at last to go out on her own.

After the war, openings for job training were scarce. Edith's father obtained a place for her to apprentice to become a hairdresser. She success-fully completed the training but never took a position because she found she didn't care for the work. There was a shortage of teachers since those who belonged to the Nazi Party were no longer permitted to teach. Edith completed several levels of training, working as she studied, and ultimately qualified to be an elementary school teacher. She taught the first four grades of school for forty years, thirty of them in the same school. She feels that the challenges and contributions of pursuing this profession have decisively shaped her life.

Edith had two sons, born before she was married. She married years later, and her husband took in her children, supported her education, and "awak-ened [her] political consciousness." He is not only her husband but her clos-est friend. He joined our conversation when we sat down to coffee and cake.

Edith lived through the Nazi years and the war as a growing child, then

through forty-five years in the communist German Democratic Republic, and now has lived for over ten years in a unified Germany. Edith believed in the ideals of communism—"no more exploitation!"—but she admits it was a utopian ideal: "In practice, it never worked." There were good times, however. Rent, transportation, and theater tickets were cheap. How has she met the changes of the past ten years? "You get used to it," she says. She and her husband are relatively lucky in having good pensions. For better or for worse, they explained, they belong to the generation that experienced everything, living under three dramatically different regimes, whereas their children know little about the past, and their grandchildren nothing.

Edith's idealism survives. "What do women of our age want?" she asks, and answers,

. . . that things go well for their families, that everyone achieves something and above all, stays healthy.

. . . that in the whole world, there is no war.

. . . that those who have a say in the world are those with the greatest knowledge and understanding, not those with the most wealth.

Patricia BORN DECEMBER 25

INTERVIEWED AND PHOTOGRAPHED JULY 12, 2000

Patricia was the first 1931 woman I met when I started this project. I was surprised that her life had differed from mine in so many ways. Despite those differences, Patricia and I have become good friends, mostly through e-mail correspondence. I have been in more frequent contact with her than with any of the other women, appreciating and admiring her independence of mind and her vivid, witty way of expressing herself. What I learned about her in my interview has been supplemented many times over by what she has told me since.

Patricia was told that it was a long and snowy drive to the hospital from Grandmother's farm in Duluth, Minnesota, and that she was born on Christmas Day with teeth and a high fever. Not expected to live, she was given a name near at hand: Sister Patricia was the head of the hospital. In later years, she was willing to deliver Meals on Wheels on her Christmas birthday, not minding that a bit since she's "not a holiday person."

Patricia was the fourth of four children. Mother and children moved back to the Czech neighborhood in Cedar Rapids, Iowa, when Patricia was still an infant. Her father, a truck driver, left the family after a time, and her parents divorced when she was ten. A couple of years later, her mother remarried to a man Patricia liked. She wrote,

> My memories have never been that we were "poor"—but I guess we were—can't recall being hungry or wanting—but my mother did work *all the time*—and maybe that is where I get my strong need to work—be self-sufficient and able to take care of myself.

Patricia's mother worked, in turn, at grocery stores, a men's clothing store, a department store in the stockroom, and at nights as a baker.

Patricia remembers playing after school with friends who lived in houses with dirt floors and kerosene lamps. On Saturdays and in the summers until she was fifteen, she went to a Bohemian school to learn the language and culture. She recalls having to memorize a Czech poem to recite in a Christmas program. She says that task was less difficult for her than the gymnastic lessons!

Patricia became known in high school for all the activities she was in. At first, she was just someone's "little sister," but she quickly made many

PAT YUVA AND BOBBYSLAX

friends. She became a cheerleader almost by accident. Voicing criticism at a cheerleading practice, she was asked to try out and was accepted. This turn of events surprised her because she hated phys ed. She remembers teachers often being "mean" and that she was once told her interpretation of a poem was "wrong." Outside of school, she was a "wheel" at the Keen Teen Klub at the Y, which drew students from all four Cedar Rapids high schools to put on plays and hold other activities. A newspaper of the time cited Pat, a member of the student council at school, as "a great committee-woman [who] has done more than her share on school and Keen Teen Klub committees."

When Patricia graduated from high school, she was mainly eager to get a job and earn her own money. Her first job was as an elevator operator in a bank, but claustrophobia drove her to the job market again. She described her early working life as consisting of numerous office jobs: "Whenever I learned a job, and there was no 'advancement,' I would go to another job." She had an early ambition to be a nurse and she twice started nursing studies but was unable to complete them, once because of illness and once because she was also working full-time.

Patricia was thirty-two when she married. That was "old" in those days, and her relatives had been worried about her prospects. She had one child, a daughter. She began her career as a medical transcriptionist when her daughter was a baby. One of the local hospitals needed a typist, and Patricia figured she could do that "even though I flunked typing class in high school." While working for the hospital, she also worked part-time in doctors' offices and as a bookkeeper. Her job as a medical transcriptionist eventually moved home since she could work there with a computer, and she works for a Virginia-based firm to this day.

Divorced at fifty-three, Patricia has remained single. She believes that she has more in common with other single or divorced women than with women who happen to be her age. In one of the many lively, stream-of-consciousness e-mails that I have received from her since we met, Patricia wrote,

> Don't know why some women marry so quickly (?) and/or often (?) . . . am not so sure I would want to go through it all again . . . guess it would, of course, depend on how emotionally challenging (or demanding) a relationship would be . . . and then there is always the thought of losing one's independence (lordy, I sound like my mother!!!!) . . .

To her, the women's movement "hasn't made that much difference." Perhaps it has, she thinks, to women with more education, who can take advantage of more opportunities. Anyway, "women know that without women, men would be nothing."

In 2000 Patricia moved her mobile home, complete with framed *New Yorker* covers, other art, and schnauzer dog, Fritz, from Marion, Iowa, to Rockford, Illinois. She wanted to be closer to her married daughter and new grandson. Fascinated with the child's developing skills and curiosity at fourteen months, she wrote me, "Wonder what he will be when he grows up!!! (and what will I be when I grow up!!!)" In 2001 she moved closer still, into a small house in a Chicago neighborhood where the "other" grandma had lived before her death. Patricia enjoys the city and finds her grandson "continually interesting . . . my first experience of watching a child grow and learn and struggle . . ." She says she "missed out on a lot of firsts" with her own daughter, who was cared for by a friend of Patricia's mother for almost the first four years of her life while Patricia worked.

Her immediate family was fairly loose, and Patricia has had little contact with her siblings as an adult. She always felt "different" from her sister and brothers, sensing that she had more "depth" and broader interests. Early in 2000, her mother died. Although their relationship had been rocky and Patricia never felt "liked" by her mother, she came back to Cedar Rapids in December 2000 to put a Christmas tree decorated with birdseed on her mother's grave.

During her Iowa years, Patricia volunteered at a nature center working with children. She also devoted sixteen years to Meals on Wheels. Every year since she left Iowa, Patricia has returned to Cedar Rapids to participate in the March of Dimes WalkAmerica with friends, as she did for years before she moved. One of her fondest memories is of taking part in the Dragon Boat Festival on the Cedar River three times as the oldest member of her team. In June 2002, she took part in a three-day walk sponsored by Avon to support cancer research, walking sixty miles and sleeping in tents. Her report of the successful completion of this adventure, sent to me and other friends, began, "Well, the little old lady did it!!!"

Phoebe BORN DECEMBER 30

INTERVIEWED JULY 11, 2001 PHOTOGRAPHED JANUARY 16, 2002

"I feel sandwiched between generations," Phoebe told me. "In many ways, my outlook, ideas, habits are more like younger women than a lot of my contemporaries."

Phoebe was born in Vienna and named Bianca but was called Bibi after the heroine in a series of children's books. In 1982 she decided to change her name legally to Phoebe because it sounded like Bibi but was a real name. The family was Jewish in origin but not in practice, a distinction that didn't matter to the Nazis. Her father, an obstetrician, was interned but later released through her mother's efforts. Meanwhile, Phoebe and her brother, five years older, had been sent to England for their safety. Phoebe remembers Nazis ripping open the hems of the dresses in her suitcase, looking for contraband, when they left.

She and her brother lived with a family and attended school in London but were then evacuated to different boarding schools outside the city. This was a separation even harder for Phoebe than being without her parents. The family was reunited in England and arrived in New York in 1940. Her father had to pass medical exams and could then practice medicine. Phoebe remembers being able to bring only one doll with her and having to leave behind her new doll carriage. In New York, her brother built her a replacement from an orange crate for her birthday.

After the wartime diet in England, Phoebe was found to be underweight and had to take cod liver oil and drink Ovaltine. "Did not like that!" she wrote. When she started school in New York, she was initially put back, possibly because of deafness in one ear from an ear infection. Later, she skipped two grades. She attended three different elementary schools because her parents moved several times within Manhattan. She liked math, art, music, and gym. She liked reading and remembers going to used book stores to buy or trade books and comic books.

Her parents divorced when Phoebe was twelve. She went with her mother by train to Reno, the divorce destination of those times. They stayed in a rooming house for the six weeks required for residency, and Phoebe spent hours at the municipal swimming pool and in the library. Back in New York after the divorce, Phoebe did housecleaning, grocery shopping, and cooking

for herself and her mother, who now worked during the day. Her brother lived with their father and his new wife.

Phoebe went to Hunter College High School and reports that she liked it "despite the bus rides." She participated in sports, student government, and the cheering squad her first year. She liked her classes but "did not need to do the homework — guess it wasn't challenging enough." She has many memories of outings with friends:

. . . Rented bicycles and went across the [Hudson] river to ride in New Jersey's Palisades Park. Went to the beach, and even Coney Island. Went to Yankee Stadium to watch a baseball game. (All on public transportation.) Followed games on the radio, listened to Frank Sinatra. High school and friends were empowering and fun!

She worked every summer at an assortment of jobs: as a "mother's helper," a counselor-in-training at a camp, a mimeograph operator, and a file clerk.

Phoebe's ambition to become a doctor was discouraged by her parents. Her mother had started to study medicine but did not finish in order to "help" her father. Phoebe then focused on becoming a chemist and went to the Massachusetts Institute of Technology to study chemistry. There were not many girls in her classes and, although some professors discriminated against her, she often felt like "one of the boys." Phoebe married after her junior year but completed her undergraduate studies on schedule in 1953.

After graduation, she worked as a junior chemist at a chemical company in Cambridge, Massachusetts, until she and her husband, a physicist, relocated to California for his work in 1956. A daughter, and then a son, were born between 1956 and 1959. Phoebe did some work at home. The family moved to the University of Wisconsin in 1960 for her husband's position, and Phoebe worked part-time in hematology at the university's medical school. In 1961 Phoebe divorced and moved back to Massachusetts with her

children. She worked as a chemist in a sequence of temporary and part-time jobs in the 1960s and then, in 1966, she began to study for a master's degree in education at Northeastern University, with the idea of teaching science in high school. Her former husband pressured her to get a full-time job, but she "took him to court for child support." She didn't complete the degree program but did get her teaching certification and taught at a few schools between 1967 and 1969, before returning to a position as a chemist at a hospital for a year.

In 1970 Phoebe remarried and her third child, a second daughter, was born the next year. She stayed home until 1976, but then her husband became seriously ill and she cared for him until he died in 1977. Her children were twenty-one, eighteen, and six years old. During her husband's illness, Phoebe returned to work as a chemist and afterward was employed for over three years at a chemical firm in the town where she lived, until the firm went out of business. While doing temp office work and sometimes living on unemployment insurance, Phoebe earned an MBA at Babson College. She hoped it would increase her employability. In 1985 she began working for DuPont as a chemist. Allergies caused her to transfer to technical writing from lab work, but she remained at DuPont until she retired in 1997. For the first several years, she worked part-time at second jobs as a cashier or secretary. Phoebe writes tersely about her working life:

No career, always thinking of children (reason for early part-time work). Companies failed, etc. Longest time was at DuPont, which was 70+ miles/day commute. Worked where I could get a job. Second job and/or overtime to help pay youngest daughter's college. Getting advanced degrees didn't help either . . . I felt discriminated against in my jobs . . . even with some male unenlightened contemporaries.

Phoebe : 169

Phoebe is still working, now on her third part-time job since "retirement." She hopes to truly retire in about a year "and do some piano playing and painting." Her present schedule is daunting. When I was trying to schedule a phone appointment, she explained that she worked from 6 to 10 A.M. and wasn't always out by 10. Then she goes to a gym class. In spring and summer, she often works in the garden in the afternoons. She also attends choir practice one evening a week and church on Sunday morning. She has taken on big sewing projects, such as making the bridesmaids' dresses for her younger daughter's wedding last year.

And then there is volunteer work—"Quite a lot!" Starting with co-op nursery school, the list includes a leading role in Parents without Partners, teaching Sunday school and singing in the choir, starting a church outreach program, setting up and coordinating homeless shelter dinners, and participating in MIT career workshops for women. She was also active in the League of Women Voters and Scouts. She adds, "I probably left some out." Her Episcopal church gave her special recognition in the Easter newsletter as a "star," quoting parish members who described her as "very giving," "selfless," and "quite a girl." More than once Phoebe has taken in children in need of a temporary home, and most recently, she gave shelter to a family with three sons and a baby.

She looks back on all the challenges she faced in her life, enumerating them:

> The trauma of the war and coming to a new country, feeling alone/ unsupported . . . the challenge of college, challenge of being a single parent and finding my strengths through groups I was in. Then having to deal with sick husband, widowhood, and finding the strength to carry on with children and home alone. Feel that my children were shortchanged because I was always struggling to cope.

Add to these challenges recent mini-strokes and foot surgery.

When Phoebe planted sunflowers outside, the birds went for the seeds without giving the flowers a chance. She stopped fighting the birds and filled her kitchen with images of sunflowers in every medium.

I, Ina BORN FEBRUARY 28

In July 2000, before I met the first woman of 1931 (Patricia), I completed my own questionnaire and filed it in the back of one of my 1931 project folders. I did not look at it again until I had finished the first draft of the last 1931 life story (Althea's). Because I did not give myself the luxury of expansiveness in my responses and most particularly because what the women have told me about themselves has stimulated my own memories and reflections, what follows are my original responses, annotated in italics.

Date of birth: February 28

Place of birth (town or country, at home or in a hospital):
Bronx, New York in a small private hospital
I was told that my life was in danger for two days and that the hospital was not quite adequate for the emergency. My birth certificate, I learned when I applied for my first passport, had only "Baby Girl" for my name. So that a name wouldn't be wasted if I died?

Birth order in family: 1/1
I was born seven years after my parents married. It was a sorrow and an embarrassment for my mother not to become pregnant. She was grossly overweight and decided to go on a strict diet because she believed that might be the problem. She did not discover that she was pregnant until her fifth month, when I was thought to be a tumor.

Number of siblings (number of brothers, number of sisters): 0
It marked my life to be an only child. While appreciating my parents and my place as an equal in the family, I regretted my status even when I was young. I am sure that some of my interpersonal inadequacies are due to never having experienced give-and-take with siblings at home. I was indulged—some might say spoiled—particularly by my father. It was always said that he treated me the same, as if I had been a boy. We went to ball games, we rode bikes in Central Park. For thoroughly urban people, that was a lot. At the same time, I was always expected to be feminine in dress and in manner. Much later, when I was responsible for my mother at the end of her life, I was grateful to be able to make decisions without possible opposition from siblings. Another woman, also an only child, expressed the same feeling.

Parents' occupations:

Mother: homemaker; worked as secretary before marriage at age twenty; hospital volunteer for twenty years, starting at age sixty.

Father: salesman for costume jewelry manufacturers

Both my parents left high school after one year. My mother worked briefly for a very imposing woman in the office of the League of Women Voters. My mother's attentiveness to correct English usage dates from that job. When she left, her letter of reference noted that she had a "rudimentary" education. She thought it a compliment until she looked it up in the dictionary. Using the dictionary was almost a religious prescription for her and then for me. Later in her life, she was a very conscientious volunteer at the hospital where she had often been a patient. My father was a good salesman because he was a born actor. In fact, an aunt of his was a famous actress in the Yiddish theater, and my father spent many evenings there as a youth while his parents staffed the box office. He loved the theater his whole life. He was too willful to learn well from authority, but he was very ambitious, imaginative, and hardworking.

Where did parents live most of their lives? At the end of their lives/now?

Born in New York City, died in New York City.

Couldn't imagine living anywhere else.

Parents' ages? Their ages at death? The years of death?

Father at seventy-six years in 1974

Mother at eighty-seven years in 1990

Father died of complications from diabetes, which he had lived with since his forties. Mother died in a hospice unit of a hospital when the iliostomy she had coped with for twenty-six years no longer functioned properly. Although I lived a thousand miles away, I was with her frequently, and continually in the last weeks of her life.

Both parents lived with serious chronic health problems since middle age. I was said to be a sickly child but have been extraordinarily lucky—because strong and healthy—in old age.

What role did your grandparents play in your life?
Whose parents were they? Where did they live?
This question was not included when I wrote my answers. It was added by the fourth interview. It is perhaps significant that I didn't think of it at first. My mother's parents were no longer alive for me (Mother was the eighth of eight children), but my father's parents lived in Brooklyn and were part of my life— but not a very significant part. It had something to do with our being a close (and closed?) little family of three and something to do with my mother's disparagement of them, particularly of my grandfather, as not sufficiently "refined." When I was ten or eleven, I badly wanted to sleep over in the Murphy bed in their apartment. There were big tearful hugs whenever we met and left each other.

What kind of elementary school did you attend?
I started school in the Bronx, but we moved to Manhattan when I was seven. I went to the same school from second through eighth grade. It was an old building directly across the street from my apartment house.
It was difficult not to leave too early for school. I would stand at the window until I saw other children coming. My mother liked the school being so close. Despite that, she would stand at the corner with an umbrella if it were raining when I was due to come home. For this I was mortified and ungrateful.

Alice, Eleanor, and Jane also went to P.S. 87 Man. (for Manhattan). What a delightful surprise it has been to discover friends from so long ago!

What kind of high school did you attend?
Very large (3,000), all girls, public school—Julia Richman High School.
It was a forbidding building, red brick with barred windows, no set-back, no architectural decoration of any kind. We were never told that Julia Richman was an educator and an early female education administrator, and Jewish besides.

I was in the Country School, described in Alice, Eleanor, Ethel, and Jane's stories. I took four years of Latin and three of French. Geometry made a "math avoider" of me for over thirty years. My future sister-in-law became my best friend in the first year. I was intrigued by the fact that she was born in Berlin, Germany. We both worked on the newspaper as our main extracurricular activity, becoming page editors. We then shot our chances for the top editing jobs by insisting that we be named co-editors in chief. We couldn't face the prospect of one of us having a higher position than the other, and those choosing the editors rejected our proposal. I went over to the literary magazine in my senior year. That issue included several of my poems and a story.

What were you like in high school? What words would have described you?
Good student, active, self-confident, competitive, conceited, Romantic (capital R)—loved Kipling's "If" and Henley's "Invictus"—social life entirely outside of school, dating
We were graded in percentages and avidly reviewed our friends' averages every marking period, competitive to the half-a-percentage point. My sister-in-law is still proud that she graduated fourth to my fifth in the class. The self-confidence was good—no Carol Gilligan phenomenon in us—but in me it shaded into overconfidence, which ill prepared me for the stiffer competition and more difficult work of college.

What about your friendships in high school?
This question was not in the questionnaire when I answered it. My high school friends meant a lot to me, and I have always regretted that our high school made no effort to keep track of us, much less to plan reunions.

In our wartime idealism, we were against social exclusiveness of any kind. Our class formed a "sorority" with the give-away name of Alpha Lambda Lambda, to which everybody automatically belonged. It only entailed trying to have movie dates or such on Saturdays with girls we wouldn't ordinarily have socialized with.

Did you have further education? In what, and in which years?
BA, Cornell University, 1952. Philosophy.
MA, University of Massachusetts, 1969. Philosophy.

MA, University of Iowa, 1981. Accounting.
This pattern has its duplicates in other women of 1931. Interruptions and changes of course . . .

What did you "want to become"? At what age?
Early in high school, said "lawyer" but it was not a developed ambition. At sixteen years, I was serious about being a poet.
In college, I would have said I wanted to become a professor of philosophy. Yet even before I entered college, I had chosen my future husband. I saw no contradiction in "wanting to become . . ." and planning an early marriage, but I didn't really think about it. Having a serious ambition that involved "making a living" never occurred to me.

Among the insights I have gained from the stories of the women of 1931, one of the most poignant is how your parents' economic situation limited your early life choices. Both of my parents had to go out to work to help support their families. Beginning in the mid-forties, my father's income was steadily increasing. When I was in high school, there was no question that I would go to college and could go away to college if I chose. To be deprived of that opportunity or to have to work full-time to attain it are sacrifices I did not have to make but with which I strongly empathize.

What was the effect of World War II on you? What are your memories?
It was the beginning of my social consciousness, my idealism. My most vivid memories are of the ending of the war (1944–45) and of thinking constantly about the hoped-for better postwar world. I remember our patriotism and the wartime propaganda in movies and popular songs. The emotional tone of those movies, those songs, influenced my emotional development, and the effects are still with me, particularly the unwelcome (to me) tendency to cry at sentimental things.
President Roosevelt's death in April 1945 was a trauma. I wept, I went to a service in an Episcopal church (because FDR was Episcopalian) as well as to the Free Synagogue with its politically engaged rabbi. If one were born in 1931—and not aware of President Hoover as an infant, Roosevelt was truly our "only" president.

176 : I, Ina

If you married, how old were you when you married? 19
We had been serious about each other for three years. We figured out to the penny—this was my husband's skill, not mine—that with our scholarships, summer job savings, his graduate assistantship, and a part-time job for me, we could afford to get married without being dependent on support from our parents. It was never in doubt that I would finish college.

How many times did you marry? once
Sometimes early marriages do work.

Did you have children? Number of children (boys, girls) and your age at birth of each
Girl when I was twenty-three; boy when I was twenty-seven
I expected, and hoped, to have more than two. When I was thirty-one, a baby was stillborn, a victim of my Rh-negative blood type, which I overoptimistically ignored.

Did you work outside the home before your children went to school?
No.
I started graduate work when my son started first grade. He asked me if I "teached or got teached" and was disappointed to think he might have so much schooling ahead of him.

Paid work experience:
Summer jobs, sales and clerical, during high school
   After marriage, part-time sales, then job as secretary to faculty member at Cornell who was directing my husband's graduate work. (I took a crash course in shorthand to "prepare" for this job and practiced to make my four-finger typing speedier.)
   Having moved, pregnant, to my husband's first teaching job, in South Hadley, Massachusetts, I worked at three part-time jobs before the baby came, earning the grand sum of $200.
   After the move to Iowa, I taught philosophy part-time for four years at a nearby liberal arts college, 1970–74.
   Tax preparer for H&R Block for five tax seasons, 1975–79

After completing my accounting studies, 1981–95 at the University of Iowa
teaching hospital in financial management and internal audit

Volunteer experience:
    In South Hadley, a civic awareness/action group, "Know Your Town"
    In our synagogue in Holyoke, Massachusetts, organized a conference on
Black-Jewish relations, 1969
    In Iowa City, nursing home "friendly visitor," 1970–73
    After retirement, hospice volunteer, 1996–present
    Hospice board member, 1998–2003
    Various arts committees

Are you retired? since 1995

Are your friends mostly your age, or older or younger?
Mostly younger but quite mixed. Have a significant friend (and fellow photographer) who is ninety-something.
A university community is marked by large numbers of young people. To live in such a community is to be able to stay in touch with changes in society and to be aware of one's own growing marginalization. A healthy thing.

I have always said that, apart from marrying and having children at "normal" ages, I have been "out of synch" for everything else I have done. I have twice been an older graduate student. In the 1960s, it was old to be, as I was, in your mid-thirties. The second time, I celebrated my fiftieth birthday in my last term. Then I began work in a junior position. My fellow students and my new colleagues were my children's age or younger. I didn't feel this age difference and tended to think that my teachers and superiors at work were older (because of their status) although they weren't. When I turned to photography in my mid-fifties, I was once again a beginner. Age is in a sense, of course, objective but the feeling of age is subjective. Many of the women have attested to this.

Your grown children—their locations, occupations, spouses' occupations, grandchildren:
Daughter—Michigan—has daughter (twenty-three years old), two sons (thirteen and ten). University professor; husband, middle-school teacher.

Son—Connecticut—has daughter (seven years old). University professor; wife, environmental engineer.

What are your present occupations and interests?
Photography—*serious interest since 1986*
Hospice—*I deeply believe in the hospice philosophy*
Russian language study—*started in 1994 in the expectation of acquiring a Russian-born daughter-in-law. Discontinued lessons in 2001. But not the daughter-in-law!*
Visual arts—literature

I omitted pool—the shooting kind, not the swimming kind—which I have played one morning a week since 1998 with a group of women at the local senior center.

What would you imagine you have in common with other women of your age?
Early marriage and birth of children
Deferral of "career"
"Catching up" in old age
If I consider the "other women of my age" as the women in this group, I see that my conjectures are not clearly confirmed. I was one of the youngest to marry. Only five others married before they were twenty.

The quotation marks around career *are my way of expressing that it was relatively unnatural or unexpected for us to aim for a career, an honorific term distinguishing it from merely a* job. *Some women did not have the luxury of a "career." They "always worked," as one women said, because they had to.*

Far from "catching up" in old age, some women are still working, willingly or from necessity, and others are happy to be retired and free from "living by the clock," as one woman said. Others have turned to other interests and activities, many of them to art, but they see themselves as doing something new and different, rather than "catching up." The concept probably reflects my own sense of taking my ambition out of mothballs.

Which things in your background and life history have been most important in making you the person you are?

Being an only child

Being Jewish

Born in a big city, lived my adult life in small towns

Married [over] fifty years

What I now see as an obvious omission here is the influence of my parents, which is not captured by "being an only child." The omission is not surprising to me. From my late teens on, I tried hard to distance what I was from what my parents had made of me, as if I had sprung full-grown from the head of Zeus like Athena. It took me a long time to realize and to appreciate all that they made possible for me, and how like both of them I am in so many ways. Other 1931 women were more forthcoming in crediting their parents or, sometimes, one parent.

"Being Jewish" is not so much a matter of religious observance, although I am more observant now than when I lived at home, unquestioning, in an overwhelmingly Jewish environment. It relates more to my "adult life in small towns" where I first realized that I belonged to a minority. It is not about discrimination, which I have not really experienced, unlike the African American women in this project. (A generation earlier, it would have been.) It is about always being something of an outsider, a status which, on balance, I perceive as positive.

"Born in a big city" should really read "born in New York City." Not any city will do! I left at seventeen. I love Iowa and need its space and air and light and calm; I have lived in Iowa for over thirty-two years, but I am still from New York. This is why it was so important to include women also from New York in this project. Having both New York and my small-town experiences is the key.

Marriage marks a person. So does being single. The woman who said she had more in common with other single women—although she had been married and divorced—than with women her age, was expressing that marking. Almost all the women said that they expected marriage. We were brought up as girls to expect to marry. If a marriage survives into the partners' old age, it has become the unseen, unreflected-upon background of one's life. In a rare poem, written after my poem-writing years, I called it the "medium" in which one lives, like air or water.

Is there anything about your life that you would not have expected when you were twenty?
This question was not in the interview form I answered, but it is easy to answer: As a snobby intellectual, I would never have expected to study and practice accounting nor to become an artist. I would never have expected to play pool! I would not have expected that friendships with women would be so important to me.

Is there anything about your present daily life (cooking, dressing, social life, hobbies, etc.) that would surprise your twenty-year-old self?
I am less casual in dress than many women, but much more than I would have anticipated.
Living in Iowa
I have been surprised at how few women had any response at all to this question. Perhaps because my parents had such definite ideas and standards about dress, I am very conscious about the revolution, dating from the 1960s, in how we present ourselves. Women couldn't wear pants to restaurants or to work until 1969. What woman today wears skirts more often than pants? At the more casual end of our wardrobe, which of those items were in our closets in the 1950s?
    At twenty I would have said, "Where's Iowa—or is that Ohio/Idaho . . . ?"

What is the story of you and smoking?
I added this question after the first interview, eliciting a response from that woman by e-mail. As for myself, I always expected to smoke since both parents did and "everybody" did because it was so wonderfully sophisticated. I never could learn to inhale without choking and so I held a borrowed cigarette from time to time but did not acquire the habit.
    Because it was so prevalent, I was surprised that only seventeen women had been smokers. That only two still smoked was less surprising.

How do you think your life would have been different if you had been born ten years earlier?
Would have been more involved in World War II
More conscious of the Depression
Less able to benefit from women's movement

If you had been born ten years later?
More likely to have pursued a career at an earlier age
More likely to be divorced
More affected by changes of late 1960s, 1970s

How has the women's movement affected your life?
It came too late to form my life expectations. Early, it caused me considerable frustration and confusion. Later, it provided me with unexpected opportunities.

The frustration and confusion were caused by the changed expectations of women and what they could aspire to do at a time in my life when I had already made many choices, choices influenced by very different expectations. At the women's college where my husband taught, I suddenly saw graduating students going directly to graduate school in large numbers, rather than aspiring to engagement-by-graduation or going to "Katie" Gibbs (a tony private secretarial school in Boston). These graduates included some who were not as good students as I had been. I felt wronged by timing. But how to change? What to do? It was not easy if you were well into your thirties, on the "middle way" of your life.

The unexpected opportunities for me were indubitable. There were virtually no women in accounting when I was of college age. When I decided on a second education in that field in 1978, it was not an issue. Women now account for more than half the business students in many institutions. Getting a job after my accounting studies was difficult because I was fifty, not because I was female.

It is almost hard to remember the subtle and not so subtle put-downs and being defined by what your husband was and did. It took a while but it changed. Alas, some young feminists were as adept at ignoring middle-aged women— who were merely some important person's wife—as men.

I was surprised by how many women answered this question by saying which gallantries (e.g., having doors opened was a favorite) they didn't want to lose. Others pointedly noted that early feminism was largely a white, middle-class phenomenon so that poor women and women of color didn't find a home in the movement.

It seems to me that interest in the subject of this book is evidence of changes in what is considered worthy of attention, and this interest is a legacy of the women's movement.

I, Ina : *183*

Coming Together

What if the women I met separately had the opportunity to come together in one place at one time? I imagine a reunion taking place *after* they had read each other's stories and looked into each other's faces in the photographs. In person, would they recognize likenesses, or would they be struck by how different they are? Across all the variation in the places where they were born, in the economic circumstances of their families and their adult lives, in their schooling and occupations, in their life experiences, did being born in 1931 give a certain shape to their lives? This was the question with which I started. Is there an answer?

I believe that the women would initially notice the differences among them, differences from the moment of birth. Twenty-four of them were born in hospitals; eighteen were born at home. All but two of the rural women were born at home, but seven of the twenty-nine city women were also born at home. Eight were only children. Would one have expected more among the Depression babies? Over one-third of the women came from families of four or more children.

Their schooling varied immensely. Five of the rural women went to one-room country schools. Two reported high school graduating classes of nine and two students, respectively. For their primary schooling, two women went to Catholic schools and all the others to public schools. Only five went to private (that is, nonstate) high schools. Two did not go to high school. Two of the seven non-American women had university educations. Of the fifteen Iowa women, seven went to college after high school and four graduated, two of them after a delay. All twenty New York women went to college after high school, and all but four graduated after the normal four-year interval. Two earned their degrees years later.

The women perceive their school accomplishments differently. Twelve described themselves as good or very good students in high school, and five volunteered their rankings at graduation, all of which were high. Only one woman hated school. Most women told stories about teachers, friends, and activities with a positive slant. Two women saw themselves as offbeat during their school years, not fitting in.

I asked, "What did you want to become?" and heard more than once that you were told, "what can a girl do?" usually followed by, "except become a teacher, a nurse, or a secretary," or possibly a librarian. In the face of such advice, many women cherished unfulfilled ambitions to become actresses, accountants, archeologists, beauticians, lawyers, poets, veterinarians, writers. Three had hoped to be physicians.

Despite actual and felt constraints, most of the women worked at primary occupations outside those "typical" ones. It is true that five became teachers. Two others were either advised to teach or aspired to do so, but they did not. Five became nurses, one of them a nurse educator and dean. Four had chosen this career early, whereas one came to it later in life. Three other women wanted to become nurses, but two of them were unable to afford the education; one changed her mind. Nine were employed in office work but perhaps only a few of them could have been considered secretaries. Five teachers, five nurses, nine office workers — nineteen women. Overlooking the fact that many additional women worked in offices at some time during their lives — working their way through college, helping out part-time when their families were starting, and so on — the majority of the women worked and, in some cases, are still working in the following occupations: accountant, college administrator, administrator in the federal government, attorney/judge, bed-and-breakfast owner, chemist, consultant, dietician, driver, editor, housecleaner, industrial engineer, insurance adjuster, journalist, medical transcriptionist, physician, poet, proofreader, salesperson, securities broker, social worker, storyteller, tax preparer.

There is a stark contrast between the American women's experiences of World War II and those of the women who lived through the war years in Great Britain, Germany, and Singapore. It is almost too obvious to mention, but the contrast is very real.

Attitudes expressed toward the women's movement ranged from rejection and dismissiveness to active commitment. Women with more education tended to express more positive attitudes. This correlation may well be, as some of the women remarked, because the movement offered more new opportunities to women who already had more education and means. The variety of attitudes here is best expressed story by story, rather than in an attempt at summary.

Having come together and remarked on the striking differences between them, the forty-one women born in 1931 might begin to see some similarities. Parents play a large role in many stories. Most spoke positively about their parents, sometimes the mother, sometimes the father, sometimes both. Mothers set examples and gave advice, often expressed in traditional sayings. Fathers expressed opinions that their daughters tended to accept and expectations they wanted to satisfy. A few women voiced negative views of their mothers, but none spoke ill of their fathers. Three mothers are still alive. Although some parents died young, most were present quite long in their daughters' lives. Ten mothers and six fathers were ninety years or older when they died.

Grandmothers, particularly maternal grandmothers, were very important to several women. Grandparents frequently lived close to or even in the same home as the woman's immediate family. Often they were the ones who set standards for achievement, who supported religious observance, and who gave warmth and affection.

Only three women never married. Most married in their twenties. Six were under age twenty and six over age thirty. Eight women have been divorced, seven widowed, and two divorced and widowed. There have been nine remarriages. Twenty-eight women are married now.

Some women volunteered comments about their spouses and marriages. When these comments were negative, I was usually asked not to repeat them. Even when I wasn't asked, I haven't — not in the women's own stories. There were comments about a "very unambitious" spouse whose wife has nonetheless "stuck by him," about a marriage of "expediency," about a marriage that was a disaster from the moment after the ceremony. I also heard about husbands who were their wives' "best friends," who accommodated themselves to their wives' changing lives, and who were positive shaping influences.

Of the women who married, most had two or three children. There are five only children. No married women were childless. There was a slight tendency for women from one- and two-child families to have more than one or two children. With one exception, women from families of five or more had, at most, three children. Most women did not work outside the home before their children went to school. A few did a modest amount of part-time work between children, while a husband was completing studies, or in anticipation of a divorce. Among the women staying home were some in apparently modest circumstances. Ten women "always worked." They include professional women, some with flexible schedules, and three for whom work was simply necessary.

Fourteen women are still working at their primary occupation. Because of changes in occupation, I had to use my judgment to determine what was "primary." In addition, thirteen women, counted as retired, are significantly active as artists, writers, public speakers, volunteers (church/synagogue, schools, community, and national nonprofit organizations), care center helpers, caregiving grandmothers, and participants in a family business.

They also dance, sing, quilt, sew, knit, play bridge, play musical instruments, garden, care for dogs, collect things, read, travel, care for family members as needed, take courses, fish, support social causes, walk for exercise, cook, and watch their diets.

I didn't ask specifically about the women's health but was often told. Four women are coping with breast cancer, three with diabetes, two with emphysema, and one with another lung disease. Also mentioned were arthritis, automobile accidents, depression, osteoporosis, and stroke. Three women volunteered their feeling of good luck at being healthy. Seventeen women have smoked at one time or another. Only two still do.

I don't claim to have a final score on the question of similarities and differences among the women's lives. What if they came together just to *look* at each other? Faces are fascinating, but of this I am sure: you can't read the life from the face. The camera's portrait and the portrait in words are two things, and they are only a "pair" if you are told they belong to each other. I know only that I am glad that I decided to photograph women of 1931 and also to move beyond photography with them, and I am grateful for their trust in permitting me to do so.

Appendix A

1 Date of birth
2 Place of birth (town or country, at home or in a hospital)
3 Birth order in family
4 Number of siblings (number of brothers, number of sisters)
5 Parents' occupations
6 Where did parents live most of their lives? At the end of their lives/now?
7 Parents' ages? Their ages at death? The years of death?
8 What role did your grandparents play in your life?
9 Whose parents were they? Where did they live?
10 What kind of elementary school did you attend?
11 What kind of high school did you attend?
12 What were you like in high school? What words would have described you?
13 What about your friendships in high school?
14 Did you have further education? In what, and in which years?
15 What did you "want to become"? At what age?
16 What was the effect of World War II on you? What are your memories?
17 If you married, how old were you when you married?
18 How many times did you marry? How old were you at subsequent marriages?
19 Did you have children? Number of children (boys, girls) and your age at birth of each
20 Did you work outside the home before your children went to school?
21 Paid work experience

22 Volunteer experience

23 Are you retired?

24 Are your friends mostly your age, or older or younger?

25 Your grown children—their locations, occupations, spouses' occupations, grandchildren

26 What are your present occupations and interests?

27 What would you imagine you have in common with other women of your age?

28 Which things in your background and life history have been most important in making you the person you are?

29 Is there anything about your life that you would not have expected when you were twenty?

30 Is there anything about your present daily life (cooking, dressing, social life, hobbies, etc.) that would surprise your twenty-year-old self?

31 What is the story of you and smoking?

32 How do you think your life would have been different if you had been born ten years earlier?

33 If you had been born ten years later?

34 How has the women's movement affected your life?

Appendix B

GEOGRAPHICAL INFORMATION AND INFORMATION

REGARDING NEW YORK EDUCATIONAL INSTITUTIONS

GERMANY

Dresden

Dresden, sometimes called the German Florence, has been renowned since the eighteenth century for its handsome baroque architecture and later for all the fine arts. It is the third largest city in eastern Germany. Its population has declined during the lifetime of the women of 1931 from approximately 650,000 to 450,000, a decline attributable to population out-migration and low birth rates. The city was utterly destroyed by Allied bombers in two nights of air raids in February 1945. The work of reconstruction, including the historically authentic restoration of old buildings and churches, is still incomplete. From the end of World War II until the unification of Germany in 1990, Dresden was part of the German Democratic Republic (East Germany).

The Dresden women of 1931 were born into the democratic Weimar Republic, lived through the Nazi period and the war, the destruction of their city, and then through forty-five years of the Communist regime, until its abrupt end. Since then, they have experienced the bumpy transition to capitalism and democracy. At the time of German unification, they were close to retirement age but retired early. They were observers of the high unemployment that came with the move to a free market economy, affecting the younger generation—perhaps their children—more than themselves. They found more goods available in the stores but at prices difficult to pay on their fixed incomes. They had to learn to adapt to less security than they had under the Communist regime and to differences between the values of that society, familiar for so long, and the values of the new society, so influenced by their former foe, West Germany.

GREAT BRITAIN

Great Britain consists of three ethnically distinct nations, of which England is the most prominent, but Scotland and Wales each have separate identities. Of the three 1931 women in Great Britain, one has lived in Wales all her life. The Welsh language is one of the distinguishing features of the culture of Wales. The movement to preserve and encourage the use of the language dates from the founding of the first Welsh political party in 1925 and is ongoing. The 1931 woman does not herself speak Welsh, but her grandchildren are being educated in Welsh-language schools. Wales is in the southwestern part of the island and has been Great Britain's main coal-mining area. It is a beautiful, hilly land abutting the sea. In 1931 its population was 2.2 million, a little less than Iowa's, and in 2000, it was the same as Iowa's, 2.9 million.

The two other 1931 women were born and grew up in or near London. One of them now lives in the county of Surrey, southwest of the London metropolitan area. She spent part of the war in the far southwest, in the county of Devon, where, coincidentally, the other woman now lives. Dawlish, the town where that second woman lives, was a well-known resort in earlier days, a favorite of Jane Austen, and notable to me when I traveled there for a rail line that appears to lie exactly at sea level.

Dunkirk

A memorable experience of those who lived on the southern coast during World War II was seeing the departure or arrival of the armada of small boats that helped to evacuate over 300,000 British and French soldiers from Dunkirk, France, when the French army collapsed in the war with Germany in June 1940.

IOWA

If Iowa is known to readers on the coasts at all, it is as a rural state, the state of tall corn. In keeping with national trends, however, the proportion of

Iowa's population actually living on farms has continually and steeply declined. That proportion was 40% in 1930 and less than 6% in 2000. Iowa's total population has hovered around 2.5 million since 1930 and stood at 2.9 million in the 2000 census.

Iowa's relative anonymity is really due to its lack of big cities with familiar names. It was and continues to be a state of numerous small towns and villages, sorted into 99 counties. In 1930 the state had 81 cities and towns qualified as "urban" by federal standards; in 2000 it had 127. In 1930 it had only one city with a population over 100,000; in 2000 it had two. By far the greatest number of cities and towns had populations of less than 10,000. In 1930, and still in 2000, there were over 800 villages with less than 2,500 in population; approximately 500 of those had fewer than 500 people.

Iowa may lack population but it has space. Its geographical area is 56,276 square miles, somewhat larger than all of New York State. That space is configured as a subtly beautiful landscape, changing through four distinct seasons, confirming the meaning of its name in the language of the Ioway tribe: beautiful land.

NEW YORK CITY
New York City, as I learned in fourth grade, consists of five boroughs: The Bronx, Brooklyn, Manhattan, Staten Island, and Queens. The boroughs are coterminous with the counties of Bronx, Kings, New York, Richmond, and Queens, respectively. If Iowa is associated in the public's mind with "rural," farming, and corn, then New York City stands for "big city," in fact, *the* big city. Yet Staten Island does not fit the "big city" mold, and although the Bronx, Brooklyn, and Queens are densely populated, Manhattan is really what we think of when we think "New York City."

The population of the five boroughs of New York City was just under 7 million in 1930, 7.5 million in 1940, 7.9 million in 1950, and just over 8 million in 2000. It was the largest city in the United States in all those years.

Hunter College High School
Hunter College High School was founded in 1869 and was the first school in the city to provide free education to girls past the eighth grade. Hunter was,

from the start, open to girls from all over the city who passed the entrance exam. The women who attended in the mid- to late 1940s appreciated that their fellow students were diverse and came from all boroughs and neighborhoods of the city. Like the other selective public high schools, Hunter was not a neighborhood school. Also like most of those selective schools at the time, it was sex-segregated.

Although Hunter High School was autonomous, it was closely associated with Hunter College and Hunter Model (Elementary) School. Hunter College started as a teacher preparatory school — a normal school — and the elementary and high schools provided the teachers in training with pupils to practice on. Until the high school moved into the building that the women of 1931 attended, it resided in one temporary location after another, fourteen in all, including a former boys' high school that had been condemned by the Housing Authority as unfit for the boys' use. After 1940, Hunter High School was on the Upper East Side of Manhattan, only a few blocks from Julia Richman High School.

Throughout the city schools during the years of our education, there were two separate classes in each year. A student entered school either in February or September, whichever was closer to her birthday. There were two graduations every year, two opportunities a year to be editor of the newspaper or elected to student government, and so on. The women of 1931 who went to Hunter graduated in five different classes. The practice of permitting brighter children to skip a term or more in elementary school contributed to that degree of dispersion in high school graduation dates among the women.

Graduating classes at Hunter in the late 1940s had 120–130 students. The total school population was between 1,000 and 1,200. Graduates of Hunter College High School were automatically eligible to attend any of the city colleges.

Julia Richman Country School

Julia Richman High School was a large public girls' high school for the neighborhood of midtown and uptown Manhattan. It was established in 1913 and named after an early female educator and school administrator. The Country School was one division of Julia Richman, consisting of approximately 300 girls out of a total of 3,000. The students were selected on the basis of an IQ test. The Country School was not in the country but was housed in the same large brick building in uptown Manhattan as the other divisions: Academic, Commercial, Cooperative, and General. I was not able to determine the origin of its name, a curious one since it was in the midst of the city.

Apparently, the Country School came into existence early in the 1940s. This is a conjecture based on the appearance in the 1946 yearbook of an administrator responsible for it. As far as I know, those of us who attended the Country School in the mid-1940s had no idea that it was quite new. Teachers in the Country School usually did not teach in other divisions. Although admission was by IQ test, acceptable grades were required to stay the course.

In 1968, Julia Richman became coed, and in 1996, it went out of existence. In an inspiring rebirth, the same brick building now houses six distinct schools, including an elementary school, a junior high school for autistic children, and four specialized high schools. The building is also used for several shared social service programs.

Colleges of the City of New York
The ten four-year colleges in New York City are now referred to under the acronym CUNY (City University of New York), but in the 1940s and 1950s, when the women of 1931 attended college, they were simply the "city colleges," and there were four of them: Brooklyn College, City College of New York (CCNY), Hunter College, and Queens College. Hunter was a women's college, and Brooklyn and Queens were coed. City College was the oldest and was a men's school until 1951, although women were able to study business and education and to attend evening classes before that. Hunter was the next oldest. Brooklyn and Queens Colleges only became full-fledged institutions open to both men and women in 1937. In the late 1940s and early 1950s, these colleges, like so many others, had many veterans of World War II as students.

Tuition was free for students who either passed an entrance examination or had a certain cumulative high school grade-point average. The colleges did not have uniform entrance requirements. They all had night as well as day sessions. The night school option was used by some of the 1931 women who had to work full-time while attending college. In the city's earlier history, going to night school was a famous route to assimilation and advancement for new immigrants. There was no difference in the value of a degree, whether it was earned in day or evening sessions, and it was a valued credential since the city colleges had a reputation for excellence.

Going to one of the city colleges meant living at home, which made college even more affordable. In turn, living at home resulted in long and sometimes complex subway and bus trips to go to classes. It was not the more carefree existence enjoyed by those of us who went away to college.

New York University

New York University is a private university that was established early in the nineteenth century. During the late 1940s and early 1950s, when women of 1931 attended, there were two campuses: one in Washington Square (Greenwich Village) and the other in University Heights in the Bronx. Only the former still exists.

SINGAPORE

Singapore is a densely populated, modern city-state of high-rise buildings and tropical parks located on the equator. In an area of only 250 square miles, its population is 3.5 million — 600,000 more people than in Iowa but less than one-half of one percent as spacious.

Singapore was part of the British Empire from early in the nineteenth century. It was occupied by the Japanese during World War II. After being granted independence from Great Britain in 1959, it was briefly united with Malaysia. It has been independent since 1965.

Singapore has been a major participant in the success story of south Asia: a prosperous and stable country ruled since independence by one political party with an emphasis on order and control. It is a multiracial country that has institutionalized the peaceful coexistence of its diverse citizens by officially recognizing the most important cultural and religious holidays and the various languages of all the major groups. Public policies have been designed to ensure the groups' political representation and social integration. The main population groups are Chinese (75%) — a diverse group in itself — Malay (15%), and Indian (6.5%).